FRANZ MEHRING

On Historical Materialism

NEW PARK PUBLICATIONS

Published by New Park Publications Ltd.,
186a Clapham High Street, London SW4 7UG

First published in 1893 as an appendix to *Die Lessing-Legende*
J. H. W. Dietz, Stuttgart

Translation and Biographical Note
Copyright © New Park Publications Ltd.,
1975

Set up, Printed and Bound
by Trade Union Labour

Distributed in the United States by:
Labor Publications Inc.,
135 West 14 Street, New York
New York 10011

ISBN 0 902030 76 0

Printed in Great Britain by
New Press (TU)
186a Clapham High Street, London SW4 7UG

Biographical Note

FRANZ MEHRING was born in the Prussian province of Pomerania in 1846. His father was a senior tax official and former officer in the Prussian army. After completing his schooling, Mehring broke with his family background and studied classics at the universities of Leipzig and Berlin. In 1869 he joined the staff of the radical-democratic Berlin daily *Die Zukunft*. In 1870 he joined with members of the Social Democratic Workers' Party in a protest against Prussian annexation of Alsace-Lorraine. Continuing as a bourgeois radical journalist, he came under the influence of Lassalle, founder of the anti-Marxist wing of German socialism. In 1875, Mehring published a polemic against the nationalist historian Treitschke, seeking to defend liberalism against reaction. But the social basis for liberalism was fast being destroyed by the rise of the German workers' movement and the retreat of the middle class into the arms of Bismarck and the Junkers.

For the next fifteen years Mehring grappled to understand these social forces in a Germany rapidly emerging as a leading imperialist power, in which fear of the working class led the bourgeoisie to yield the state power to the aristocratic military-bureaucratic caste. Between 1877 and 1880 Mehring wrote a number of anti-socialist articles which appeared as a book. For this he received his doctorate from Leipzig University in 1882. But in the same year he took up the defence of the social democrats against Bismarck's anti-socialist laws. While the SPD and the social-democratic press were banned, Mehring's sympathy for their rights forced him more and more to move away from his liberal standpoint and to study intensively the works of Marx and Engels.

When he finally joined the now legal SPD in 1891, he began work for *Neue Zeit* and made many important contributions on history, philosophy and literature. The essay 'On Historical Materialism' — here translated into English for the first time — was written as an answer to critics of his first major work for the Party, *The Lessing Legend*. Engel's letter to Mehring welcoming its publication in book form is appended here. In 1897-8 Mehring published, at the request of the Party, his history of German Social Democracy. At the same time he was becoming involved in the fight against the growth of revisionism in the SPD and the attempts to replace Marxism with neo-Kantianism. As part of this fight he began to publish, in 1902, the early writings of Marx and Engels, which he was the first to rediscover. Mehring was now one of the leaders of the SPD left wing, fighting against the corrosion of the Party by reformism. Between 1906 and 1911 he was a lecturer at the Party School in Berlin, where many of the later leaders of the German Communist Party began their theoretical training.

As the war approached, the struggles inside the SPD became sharper. In 1913 Mehring's former friend, Kautsky, forced him to leave his post on *Neue Zeit*. When the degeneration of the SPD leadership became open betrayal on the outbreak of the First World War, Mehring was one of the first to fight against their support of the Kaiser's war machine. Together with Rosa Luxemburg he founded *Die Internationale* in 1915, and played a leading role in its production, when Rosa was in prison and Karl Liebknecht in the army. In 1916 the seventy-year-old Mehring was himself imprisoned for four months. In 1917 he stood for one of the Berlin seats and was elected to the Prussian Parliament by a big majority. In 1918 he fought to express the support of the German working class for the Russian Revolution. In the same year, his classic work *Karl Marx: the story of his life* was published.

His last weeks of activity, in November and December 1918, were devoted to helping to found the German Communist Party, although by the time of its founding conference in January he was too ill to attend. He died on January 29 1919, soon after the murder of his comrades Luxemburg and Liebknecht, fighting as a revolutionary to the end.

On Historical Materialism

The bourgeois world today regards historical materialism as it did Darwinism a lifetime ago, and socialism half a lifetime ago. It reviles it without understanding it. Eventually, and with great difficulty, the bourgeoisie began to grasp that Darwinism was really something other than an 'ape theory', and that socialism was not a matter of 'having a share-out' or 'laying a thieving hand on all the fruits of a thousand years of culture'. But historical materialism still remains something upon which they pour phrases that are as foolish as they are cheap, describing it, for example, as the 'fantasy' of a few 'talented demagogues'.

In fact the materialist study of history is of course subject to the very laws of historical motion that it itself lays down. It is the product of historical development; it could not have been imagined in any earlier period by even the most brilliant mind. The secret of the history of mankind could only be unveiled when a certain historical level had been reached.

But while in all earlier periods the investigation of these driving causes of history was almost impossible — on account of the complicated and concealed interconnections between them and their effects — our present period has so far simplified these interconnections that the riddle could be solved. Since the establishment of large-scale industry, that is, at least since the European peace of 1815, it has been no longer a secret to any man in England that the whole political struggle there turned on the claims to supremacy of two classes: the landed aristocracy and the bourgeoisie (middle class). In France, with the return of the Bourbons, the same fact was perceived; the historians of the Restoration period, from Thierry to Guizot, Mignet and Thiers, speak of it everywhere as the key to the understanding of all French history since the Middle Ages. And since 1830 the working class, the proletariat, has been recognized in both countries as a third competitor for power. Conditions had become so simplified that one would have had to close one's eyes deliberately not to see in the fight of these three great classes and in the conflict of their interests the driving force of modern history — at least in the two most advanced countries.[1]

Thus wrote Engels about the culminating point of historical development which first awoke an understanding of the materialist conception of history in him and Marx. How this understanding was further developed can be read in Engels' works themselves.

The life work of Marx and Engels is based throughout on historical materialism; all their writings are founded upon this. It is simply a trick of the bourgeois pseudo-sciences to pretend that they made only occasional excursions into the science of history in order to find support for a theory of history which they had 'sucked out of their thumbs'. *Capital,* as Kautsky has already stressed, is in the first place an historical work, and indeed, in relation to history, it is a mine of only partially explored treasures. And in just the same way one can say that the writings of Engels are incomparably richer in content than they are in scope, encompassing infinitely more historical material than is dreamt of by the academics, who take a few partially understood or deliberately misunderstood sentences at face value, and then think they have done something wonderful in discovering a 'contradiction' or something of the sort in them. It would be a very worthwhile task to bring together the wealth of historical views which are scattered in the works of Marx and Engels in a systematic fashion, and certainly this task will at some point be carried out. But for now we must content ourselves with a general indication, because my aim here is to draw only the essential outlines of historical materialism, and to do so in a negative rather than a positive way, through the refutation of the commonest objections which are raised against it.[2]

Karl Marx himself summed up historical materialism briefly and convincingly in his foreword to the *Critique of Political Economy,* which was published in 1859. He says there:

> The general conclusion at which I arrived and which, once reached, became the guiding principle of my studies can be summarized as follows. In the social production of their existence, men inevitably enter into definite relations, which are independent of their will, namely relations of production appropriate to a given stage in the development of their material forces of production. The totality of these relations of production constitutes the economic structure of society, the real foundation, on which arises a legal and political superstructure and to which correspond

definite forms of social consciousness. The mode of production of material life conditions the general process of social, political and intellectual life. It is not the consciousness of men that determines their existence, but their social existence that determines their consciousness. At a certain stage of development, the material productive forces of society come into conflict with the existing relations of production or — this merely expresses the same thing in legal terms — with the property relations within the framework of which they have operated hitherto. From forms of development of the productive forces these relations turn into their fetters. Then begins an era of social revolution. The changes in the economic foundation lead sooner or later to the transformation of the whole immense superstructure. In studying such transformations it is always necessary to distinguish between the material transformation of the economic conditions of production, which can be determined with the precision of natural science, and the legal, political, religious, artistic or philosophic — in short, ideological forms in which men become conscious of this conflict and fight it out. Just as one does not judge an individual by what he thinks about himself, so one cannot judge such a period of transformation by its consciousness, but, on the contrary, this consciousness must be explained from the contradictions of material life, from the conflict existing between the social forces of production and the relations of production. No social order is ever destroyed before all the productive forces for which it is sufficient have been developed, and new superior relations of production never replace older ones before the material conditions for their existence have matured within the framework of the old society. Mankind thus inevitably sets itself only such tasks as it is able to solve, since closer examination will always show that the problem itself arises only when the material conditions for its solution are already present or at least in the course of formation. In broad outline, the Asiatic, ancient, feudal and modern bourgeois modes of production may be designated as epochs marking progress in the economic development of society. The bourgeois mode of production is the last antagonistic form of the social process of production — antagonistic not in the sense of individual antagonism but of an antagonism that emanates from the individuals' social conditions of existence — but the productive forces developing within bourgeois society create also the material conditions for a solution of this antagonism. The pre-history of society accordingly closes with this social formation.[3]

In these few words, the law of motion of human history is exhaustively presented with a profound clarity and lucidity unparalleled in any other writings. And it really takes a professor of philosophy from the fair lake city of Leipzig to find in them, as Mr. Paul Barth does, 'vague words and images', very vague formulations of social statics and dynamics patched together out of imagery. In so far however as human beings are the bearers of historical development, Marx and Engels had already described them as such eleven years earlier in the *Communist Manifesto:*

> The history of all hitherto existing society is the history of class struggles. Freeman and slave, patrician and plebeian, lord and serf, guild master and journeyman, in a word, oppressor and oppressed, stood in constant opposition to one another, carried on an uninterrupted, now hidden, now open fight that each time ended, either in a revolutionary re-constitution of society at large, or in the common ruin of the contending classes. In the earlier epochs of history, we find almost everywhere a complicated arrangement of society into various orders, a manifold gradation of social rank. In ancient Rome we have patricians, knights, plebeians, slaves; in the Middle Ages, feudal lords, vassals, guild-masters, journeymen, apprentices, serfs; in almost all of these again, subordinate gradations. The modern bourgeois society that has sprouted from the ruins of feudal society has not done away with class antagonisms. It has but established new classes, new conditions of oppression, new forms of struggle in place of the old ones. Our epoch, the epoch of the bourgeoisie, possesses, however, this distinctive feature: it has simplified the class antagonisms. Society as a whole is more and more splitting up into two great hostile camps, into two great classes directly facing each other: Bourgeoisie and Proletariat.[4]

This is followed by the famous description of how the bourgeoisie on the one hand, and the proletariat on the other, have to develop according to the conditions of their historical existence, a description which has stood the test of almost half a century of unprecedented upheavals brilliantly; it is followed by the proof of why and how the proletariat will be victorious over the bourgeoisie. With the overthrow of the old conditions of production, the proletariat will negate the class opposites, the classes themselves, and with them its own rule as a class. 'In the place of the old bourgeois society, with its classes and class opposites, comes an association, in which the free development of each will be the condition of the free development of all.'

And we should add here some of the things that Engels said at the grave of his friend:

> Just as Darwin discovered the law of development of organic nature, so Marx discovered the law of development of human history: the simple fact, hitherto concealed by an overgrowth of ideology, that mankind must first of all eat, drink, have shelter and clothing, before it can pursue politics, science, art, religion, etc.; that therefore the production of the immediate material means of subsistence and consequently the degree of

economic development attained by a given people or during a given epoch form the foundation upon which the state institutions, the legal conceptions, the ideas on art, and even on religion, of the people concerned have been evolved, and in the light of which they must, therefore, be explained, instead of vice versa, as had hitherto been the case.[5]

A simple fact indeed — in the spirit of Ludwig Feuerbach, who said on this subject: 'It is a specific mark of a philosopher that he is not a professor of philosophy. The simplest truths are those that men take the longest time to reach.' Feuerbach was the link between Hegel and Marx, but he was halted half way by the miserable circumstances that predominated in Germany at the time; he considered the 'arrival at Truth' still as a purely ideological process. But Marx and Engels did not 'arrive at' historical materialism in this way, and to say in their praise that they spun it out of their heads would be an insult to them. Because even with the best of intentions it would mean declaring the whole materialist conception of history to be an invention conjured up out of empty fantasy. Much rather, the real fame of Marx and Engels consists in having given, with historical materialism itself, the most striking proof of its correctness. They did not only, as did Feuerbach, have a knowledge of German philosophy, but also of the French Revolution and British industry. They solved the riddle of human history when this task was only just being presented to mankind, when the 'material conditions' for its solution were still very much involved 'in the process of their becoming'. And they proved themselves as thinkers of the first order, when they recognized almost fifty years ago, from relatively faint signs, what the bourgeois scientists of all countries, despite the immeasurable wealth of very clear evidence, are not even able to grasp today, and of which they have at the most only an occasional inkling.

I should like to give a very remarkable example of how little is achieved by hatching out any odd theoretical proposition for polemical purposes, though it may sound extraordinarily illuminating, agree perfectly in expression and content with scientific knowledge, and result from a penetrating study of historical development. We must thank the goodness of Herr Professor Lujo Brentano for the reference to the fact that the historical school of romanticism came very close to a materialist conception of history, namely in relation to a passage by Lavergne-Peguilhen, which runs as follows:

> Perhaps the social sciences as such have made so little progress, because the economic forms themselves have not been sufficiently differentiated,

because it has not been understood that they constitute the whole basis of the social and state organizations. It is not considered that production and the distribution of products, culture and its diffusion, state legislation and the form of the state must derive their content and development entirely out of the economic forms; that these important factors in the history of society stem just as unavoidably from the economic forms, and their appropriate application, as the product from the creative interaction of productive forces, and that where there are social ills, these in general have their source in the contradiction between the forms of society and the forms of the state.[6]

This was written in the year 1838, by a renowned representative of this historical romantic school, the same school which Marx subjects to such annihilating criticism in his *Deutsch-Französische Jahrbücher*. And yet, if you disregard the fact that Marx did not derive production and distribution from the economic forms, but on the contrary, he derives the economic forms from production and distribution, he appears at first glance to have copied Lavergne-Peguilhen in the materialist theory of history.

However, what counts is the 'appropriate utilization'. The historical romantic school was a reaction against classical bourgeois political economy, which declared the forms of production of the bourgeois classes as the only natural form, and the economic forms of these classes to be eternal laws of nature. Against these exaggerations historical romanticism turned, in the interests of the Junkers, to the patriarchal glorification of the dependent economic relationships of the landlords and the bondsmen; the demand of the liberal school for political freedom was opposed by the proposition that the real constitution of a people was not a few pages of laws and statutes, but the economic power relations, that is in the given case, the master-and-servant relationships which were left over from the feudal period. The theoretical struggle between bourgeois political economy and historical romanticism was the ideological reflection of the class struggle between the bourgeoisie and the Junkers. Each of the two tendencies declared that the form of production and economy which suited its own class was an eternal, natural, unchanging law; the fact that the liberal, vulgar economists used abstract illusions, that the historical romantics relied on brutal facts, that the one had a more idealistic appearance, the other a materialistic one, only came from the difference between the historical development of the classes in struggle. The bourgeoisie was still striving to become the ruling class, and thus painted its coming period of rule as the state of general happiness; the Junkers were the ruling class and had to be satisfied with romantically idealizing the relations of economic dependence on which their power rested.

Lavergne-Peguilhen's statement too amounts to nothing more than such a glorification. He is simply trying to say: the feudal forms of society should be the basis for the whole of the social and state organization; the form of the state and the making of laws are to be derived from them; if they depart from them, then society becomes diseased. Lavergne-Peguilhen, in the exposition he derives from his proposition, makes no secret of his intentions. He differentiates between three forms of economic organization which follow each other and from now on 'intermingle': an economy based on force, a 'shared' economy, and a money economy, which correspond to the state forms of despotism, aristocracy and monarchy; and the moral feelings of fear, love and egoism. What he calls the 'shared' economy, the aristocracy, or, to call the thing by its right name, feudalism — is love. 'The material exchange of mutual services', writes Lavergne-Peguilhen, word for word, 'is everywhere, the source of love and devotion.' But since history had the mistaken idea of obscuring these sources and of 'mixing' the economic forms, so Lavergne-Peguilhen wants to 'mix' the forms of the state, of course with 'appropriate utilization'. The aristocracy is to rule in the 'local government system', 'with the power that the richer and better educated members of the community have to exercise both as community legislators and as administrators over the great mass of their disenfranchised protégés in the community.' Alongside this a part of despotism is to remain, which 'even in its most extreme form hardly destroys the social forces as much as the "tyranny of law" '; and also a part of monarchy, but without 'self-interest', and instead 'encompassing all interests with the same love, from its sublime standpoint'. It becomes clear after this what Lavergne-Peguilhen is aiming at: the restoration of the rule of the feudal lords, and 'the King absolute, if he carries out their will'. His work is already criticized in the *Communist Manifesto*, in its judgment of 'feudal socialism': which '. . . sometimes strikes the bourgeoisie in the heart, through bitter and witty judgment, which appears funny through its complete inability to understand the course of modern history.' Only the second part of this judgment of the German romantics is even more to the point than the first. Their defeat by the bourgeoisie had already taken place, and had sharpened the wits of the feudal socialists in France and England. This had given them a dim intimation that the 'old phrases of the restoration period had become impossible'; while German and particularly Prussian feudalism was still happily in power and could, in opposition to the encroachments on its preserves of the Stein-Hardenberg legislation, which was in no sense decisive, inscribe on its banner a medieval feudalism disguised in moralistic commonplaces but otherwise undiminished.

It is just this inability to understand, even in a superficial way, any economic form other than the feudal one which characterizes the historical romantic school, but because, in their narrow class interests, they sought to permeate every legal, state, religious or other relation on heaven and earth with this one economic form, so they occasionally hit upon phrases which from a distance sound like dialectical materialism, even though they in fact stand as far from it as selfish class interest from scientific knowledge. Lavergne-Peguilhen stood in a similar relation to Marx and Engels as Gerlach and Stahl did to Lassalle twenty years later. In the Prussian Senate (*Landratskammer*) Gerlach has often enough upheld, in his own peculiar manner, Lassalle's later constitutional theory against the liberal opposition. But Lassalle himself, in his 'System of Acquired Rights', had delivered the scientific *coup de grâce* to these last offshoots of historical romanticism.

This school thus has nothing to do with historical materialism — or to stretch a point, it might have had to the extent that its blatant class ideology was part of the ferment through which Marx and Engels came to the materialistic theory of history.

But even this was not the case. Before I had been able to see the whole of his now justifiably forgotten work, I thought Lavergne-Peguilhen's proposition striking enough to be worth sending to Engels with a query as to whether he or Marx had known the writers of the historical romantic school — Marwitz, Adam Mueller, Haller, Lavergne-Peguilhen, etc. — and been influenced by them. Engels had the great kindness to reply on September 28 [1892 — *Ed.*]:

> I have Marwitz's *Inheritance* myself and read the book through a few years ago but I discovered nothing in it except superb things about cavalry and an unshakeable belief in the miraculous power of five blows of the whip when administered by nobleman to plebeian. Otherwise I have remained an entire stranger to this literature since 1841-42 — I pay only the most superficial attention to it — and I certainly owe absolutely nothing to it in

the field in question. Marx had acquainted himself in his Bonn and Berlin days with Adam Mueller and Herr von Haller's *Restauration,* etc.; he spoke only with considerable contempt of this insipid, bombastic, verbose imitation of the French romanticists Joseph de Maistre and Cardinal Bonald. But even if he had come across passages like the one cited from Lavergne-Peguilhen they could not have made the slightest impression upon him at that time if he understood at all what those people wanted to say. Marx was then a Hegelian and that passage was pure heresy to him. He knew nothing whatever about political economy and could not have had any idea about the meaning of a term like *Wirtschaftsform,* (economic form). Hence the passage in question, even *if* he had known it, would have gone in one ear and come out the other without leaving a perceptible trace in his memory. But I greatly doubt whether traces of such views could have been found in the works of the romantic historians which Marx read between 1837 and 1842.

The passage is of course exceedingly noteworthy but I would like to have the quotation verified. I do not know the book, but its author is familiar to me as an adherent of the 'historical school'. The passage deviates in two points from the modern conception: 1) in deducing production and distribution from the form of economy instead of conversely deducing the form of economy from production; and 2) in the role which it assigns to the 'appropriate utilization' of the form of economy, which one may take to mean anything conceivable until one learns from the book itself what the author has in mind.

However the most peculiar thing is that the correct conception of history is to be found *in abstracto* among the very people who have been distorting history most *in concreto,* theoretically as well as practically. These people might have seen in the case of feudalism how *here* the form of state evolves from the form of economy because things are clear and unconcealed here, as if so to speak lying on the palm of your hand. I say they *'might have'* because apart from the above unverified passage — you say yourself it was *given* to you — I have never been able to discover more about it than that evidently the theoreticians of feudalism are less abstract than the bourgeois liberals. If now one of these goes further and generalizes this conception of the interconnection between the spread of culture and the form of state on the one hand and the form of economy within feudal society on the other by extending it to *all* forms of economy and state, how explain after that the total blindness of the same romanticist as soon as *other* forms of economy are at issue, for instance, the bourgeois form of economy and the forms of state corresponding to its various stages of development: medieval guild commune, absolute monarchy, constitutional monarchy, republic? It is hard to make this hang together. And the man who considers the form of economy to be the basis of the entire social and governmental organization belongs to a school to which the absolute monarchy of the seventeenth and eighteenth centuries already signifies the fall of man, a betrayal of the true doctrine of the state.

True it says moreover that the form of state is brought forth just as inevitably by the form of economy and its *appropriate utilization* as the child is brought forth by the sexual union of man and woman. In consideration of the world-famed doctrine of the school to which the author belongs I can explain this only as follows: The true form of economy is the feudal one. But inasmuch as the malice of man conspires against it it must be 'appropriately utilized' in such a way that its existence may be safe against these attacks and preserved for all eternity and that the 'form of state', etc., may forever correspond to it, i.e., should be retrojected if at all possible to the thirteenth or fourteenth century. Then the best of worlds and the finest of historical theories would equally be realized and the Lavergne-Perguilhenian generalization would be reduced again to its true content: that feudal society begets a feudal political system.[7]

Thus wrote Engels. And as we verified the quotation according to his wishes, and dug up Lavergne-Peguilhen's book to find the relationship explained above, we could only thank him for his informative explanation, that out of a single bone, he had correctly reconstructed the whole feudal mastodon.

We should now deal with two of the commonest objections that are associated with the name of historical materialism. Idealism and materialism are the opposing replies to the great basic philosophical question as to the relationship between thinking and being, the question whether mind or nature came first.

In and for themselves they have nothing at all to do with moral ideals. Such ideals can be cherished by the philosophical materialist to the highest and purest degree, while the philosophical idealist does not need to possess them in the least. But after the long years of anti-clericalism, the word materialism has had another meaning attached to it, insinuating immorality, and frequently tending to creep into the works of bourgeois science.

By the word materialism, the philistine understands gluttony, drunkenness, lust of the eye, lust of the flesh, arrogance, cupidity, avarice, covetousness, profit hunting and stock exchange swindling — in short, all the filthy vices in which he himself indulges in private. By the word idealism, he understands the belief in virtue, universal philanthropy, and in general, a 'better world' of which he boasts before others but in which he himself at the utmost believes only as long as he is undergoing the hangover or bankruptcy consequent upon his customary 'materialist' excesses. It is then that he sings his favourite song, 'What is man? — Half beast, half angel'.[8]

If one wants to use the words in this metaphorical sense, then it must be said that today the profession of historical materialism demands a high moral idealism, since it invariably brings with it poverty, persecution and slander, whereas every careerist makes historical idealism his cause, since it offers the richest expectations of all earthly goods, of happiness, of fat sinecures, of all possible decorations of merit, titles and honours. We are in no way saying that all idealist historians are motivated by sordid reasons, but we should be allowed to reject every immoral blemish which is attached to historical materialism, as a foolish and impudent aspersion.

More easily understood, although equally a gross mistake, is the confusion between historical materialism and the materialism of the natural sciences. The latter overlooks the fact that man does not only live in nature, but also in society, that there is not only natural but also social science. Historical materialism encompasses the materialism of the natural sciences, but not the other way around. The materialism of the natural sciences sees man as a consciously acting creation of nature, but does not study how the consciousness of man is determined within human society. So when it ventures into the field of history, it turns into its sharpest opposite, into the most extreme idealism. It believes in the spiritual magic force of great men, who make history; we remember Buechner's adulation of Friedrich II, and Haeckel's idolizing of Bismarck, which was coupled with the most absurd hatred for socialists. It knows only about ideal driving forces within human society. A real pattern for this species is Hellwald's *History of Culture*. Its author does not see that the religious reformation of the sixteenth century was only the ideological reflection of an economic movement, but rather: 'The reformation had an extraordinary influence on the economic changes.' He does not notice that the requirements of trade led to standing armies and trade wars, but rather: 'The growing search for peace was the cause of the standing armies and later indirectly caused new wars.' He does not understand the economic necessity for an absolute monarchy in the seventeenth and eighteenth centuries, but rather: 'It must be stated that the despotism of Louis XIV, the regime of court minions and mistresses would never have been possible, if the people had used their veto against it, because in the last instance all the power lies with them.'[9]

And so on indefinitely. On almost every one of its 800 pages, Hellwald makes similar or even worse blunders. Faced with this kind of 'materialist' writing of history, the idealist historians have, of course, easy game. But they should not make historical materialism responsible for Hellwald and his comrades. The materialism of the natural sciences then arrives at the greatest illogicality through what appears to be the greatest logical consistency. In that it sees man only a consciously acting animal, it makes history into a senseless patchwork of ideal motives and purposes; because it wrongly assumes consciously acting man to be an isolated creation of nature, it reaches the idealistic spectre of a history of humanity which rushes like a mad shadow dance through the material relations of eternal nature. Historical materialism instead starts from the scientific fact that man is not simply an isolated animal, but rather a social animal, that he reaches consciousness only in the community of social groupings (tribe, gens, class) and can live in it only as a conscious human being, so that the material basis of these groupings determines his ideal consciousness and their progressive development represents the driving forces of human history.[10]

So much for what has been grafted onto historical materialism, abusing its good name. This exhausts a large part of the objections which have been raised. As for an objective critique of the materialist conception of history — apart from an attempt which I am about to mention — bourgeois science has never carried this out. With what foolish talk the most 'exemplary' representatives of this science seek to clamber over the uncomfortable impediment formed by their own idealizations and embellishments, intended to reassure bourgeois class consciousness! One can be convinced of this many times over in the lecture in which Mr. Adolf Wagner, the 'foremost teacher of social economy at the best of the German universities', further illumined the already enlightened men of the Protestant Social Congress in the year 1892.[11]

Although we do not in any way place all the representatives of bourgeois science on the same level as this professional sophist and sycophant, we have, despite years of observation of the criticism of historical materialism, discovered nothing in them apart from general phrases, which are less objective criticisms than moral reproaches. They say, more or less, that historical materialism is an arbitrary construction of history which squeezes the uncommonly manifold life of humanity into a bare formula: that it denies all ideal forces, that it makes humanity into a helpless plaything of a mechanical development, and that it rejects all moral standards.

Of all this precisely the opposite is true. Historical materialism finishes off every arbitrary construction of history; it eliminates all bare formulas, that try to treat the varied life of humanity all alike. 'The materialist method turns into its opposite, if it is not used as the guide in historical studies, but rather as a finished pattern, to which one cuts historical events'.[12]

Thus Engels, and similarly Kautsky, protested against every attempt to make historical materialism superficial as if there were only ever two camps, two classes in mutual conflict, homogeneous masses, the revolutionary and the reactionary mass. 'If this was in fact the case, then the writing of history would be quite an easy thing. But in reality, the relations are not so easy. Society is and will become even more, an incredibly complicated organism, with the most different classes and the most different class interests, which according to the form of things, can group themselves in the most different of parties.'[13]

Historical materialism approaches every section of history without any preconceptions; it simply examines it from its basis to its highest point, starting from its economic structure, rising to its spiritual conceptions.

But, it is said, this is precisely the 'arbitrary historical construction'. How do you know that economics is the basis of historical development, instead of philosophy? Now, we know it from this, that men must be able to eat, drink, live and must clothe themselves first before they can think and write poetry, that man only reaches consciousness through his social relations with other men, and that accordingly, his consciousness is determined through his social being, and not the reverse, his social being through his consciousness. Precisely the assumption that men only come to eat, drink and live from thought, that they only come to economics from philosophy, is precisely the most obviously 'arbitrary' assumption, and accordingly historical idealism leads to the most astounding 'historical constructions'. Even stranger — or perhaps not so strange — the modern epigones of historical idealism admit this in a certain sense in that they never tire of making fun of the 'historical constructions' of its greatest representative, that is Hegel. But it is not the 'historical construction' of Hegel, in which they outdo him a thousand times, that annoys them, but rather Hegel's scientific conception of history as a process of human development, whose gradual climb through all detours and confused paths must be followed, and whose inner laws must be proved through all apparent contingencies. This great thought, the most mature fruit of our classical philosophy, the rebirth of the old Greek dialectic, was taken over by Marx and Engels from Hegel: 'We German socialists are proud of the fact that we come from not only Saint Simon, Fourier and Owen, but also from Kant and Hegel.'[14] But they recognized that Hegel, despite many brilliant glimpses into the course of historical development, arrived only at 'arbitrary constructions of history', because he took the effect to be the cause, things to be the reflections of ideas, and not, as it really is, ideas the reflections of things.

For Hegel, this conception was very natural, since the bourgeois classes in Germany had in no way achieved a real life of their own; they had to flee into the ethereal heights of ideas, in order to secure an independent existence, and here they fought out their revolutionary battles in forms which were unobjectionable to the absolutist-feudal reaction, or only as slightly irritating as possible. Hegel's dialectical method, which presents the whole natural, historical and spiritual world as a process, caught in constant movement and development, and attempts to prove the inner relations of this movement and development, finishes nevertheless with a system, which discovered the absolute idea in the estate monarchy, an idealism in the blue Hussars, a necessary condition in the feudal lords, a deep meaning in original sin, a category in the crown princes, and so on.

But as soon as a new class arose out of the German bourgeoisie in the course of economic development and entered into the class struggle, that is the proletariat, then it was natural that this new class tried to fight once again with its feet on the ground, and that it accordingly approached its maternal inheritance with some reservation, taking the revolutionary content from bourgeois philosophy, but discarding its reactionary form. We have already seen that the spiritual pioneers of the proletariat placed Hegel's dialectic on its feet, instead of leaving it standing on its head. 'To Hegel, the thought process of the human brain, which under the name of "The Idea" he even transforms into an independent subject, is the demi-urge of the real world, and the real world is only the external, phenomenal form of "The Idea". With me, on the contrary, the ideal is nothing else than the material world reflected by the human mind and translated into forms of thought.' (Marx). But in this Hegel was also finished as far as the bourgeois world was concerned which had been able to happily forget the revolutionary content of his dialectic thanks to its reactionary form. 'In its mystified form the dialectic became the fashion in Germany, because it seemed to transfigure and glorify the existing state of things. In its rational form it is a scandal and an abomination to bourgeoisdom and its doctrinaire professors, because it includes in its comprehension and affirmative recognition of the existing state of things, at the same time also, the recognition of the negation of that state, of its inevitable breaking up; because it regards every historically developed social form in fluid movement, and therefore takes into account its transient nature no less than its momentary existence; because it lets nothing impose on it, and is in its essence critical and revolutionary.' And Hegel has in fact become a vexation and abomination for the German bourgeoisie not because of his weakness, but rather because of his strength, not because of his 'arbitrary historical constructions', but because of his dialectical method. Because only the latter dances the dance of death for the bourgeoisie, but not the former.

Consequently, they had to make a clean sweep with all of Hegel, and the foremost philosopher of the German petty-bourgeoisie also drew this conclusion. Schopenhauer rejected the whole of the 'charlatan' Hegel; above all he rejected Hegel's philosophy of history. He did not see any progressive process of development in the history of humanity; he only saw in it a history of individuals; the German petty-bourgeois, whose prophet he was, is the same person he was from the very beginning and will be in the future. Schopenhauer's philosophy reached its highest point in the 'insight, that at all times, the same was, is and will be.' He writes: 'History shows on all sides, only the same thing, except in different forms: the chapters of the history of humanity are basically only different in name and the dates; the really essential content is the same everywhere... the material of history is the individual in his solitude and fortuitousness, what always is, and then is not, forevermore, the fleeting intertwining like clouds in the wind of moving humanity, which so often can be transformed completely, through the slightest chance.' So closely comes Schopenhauer's philosophical idealism to mechanical materialism in its conception of history. In fact they are opposite poles of the same narrow outlook. And when Schopenhauer said grimly of the materialism of the natural sciences: 'These gentlemen of the crucible must be taught that simple chemistry makes one capable of being a chemist but not a philosopher', so he should be taught that simple philosophizing makes one capable of sneaking about, but not of historical investigation. However Schopenhauer was consistent in his own fashion, and as soon as he had thrown away Hegel's dialectical method, then he had to throw away Hegel's historical constructions with it.

In the meantime, the more the German petty bourgeoisie developed into a large industrial bourgeoisie, the more this bourgeoisie in the class struggle abjured its own ideals, and plunged back into the shadows of feudal absolutism, the more grew their need to prove the historical reason for this peculiar crablike progress. And since Hegel's dialectic had to be a vexation and an abomination to them for the reasons that Marx mentions, so they were left only with Hegel's historical constructions. Their historians discovered the absolute idea in the German Reich, an ideal in militarism, a deep significance in the exploitation of the proletariat by the bourgeoisie, a necessary condition in the bank rate, a category in the Hohenzollern dynasty and so on. And in its stupid crafty shopkeepers' way, the bourgeoisie claims to realize bourgeois idealism, while they throw accusations of 'arbitrary historical construction' at the real saviour of what was meaningful and great in their idealism. So the Gracchi bewail the tumult once again, and what kind of Gracchi they are!

Let us glance once again at the accusations and objections which have been made against historical materialism: that it denies all ideal forces, that it makes humanity the helpless plaything of a mechanical development, that it rejects all moral standards.

Historical materialism is no closed system crowned by an ultimate truth; it is the scientific method for the investigation of processes of human development. It starts from the unchallengeable fact, that human beings do not only live in nature but also in society. There have never been people in isolation; every man who accidentally loses contact with human society, quickly starves and dies. But historical materialism thus recognizes all ideal forces in the widest context. 'Of everything that happens in nature, nothing happens as a desired, conscious purpose. On the other hand, in the history of society, the participants are nothing but human beings endowed with consciousness, acting with thought and passion, working for specific purposes; nothing happens without a conscious intention, without a planned goal. . . . Will is determined through thought or passion. But the levers which in turn determined the passion or the thought are of very different kinds. They can be outside objects or ideal motives, greed, "enthusiasm for truth and justice", personal hatred or just individual peculiarities of all kinds' (Engels). This is the essential difference between the history of the development of nature on the one hand and of society on the other. But apparently all the innumerable conflicts of individual actions and wills in history only lead to the same result as the unconscious, blind agencies in nature. On the surface of history accident seems to reign as much as on the surface of nature. 'Only rarely does what is desired take place; in most cases, the desired aims cut across each other, and come into conflict, or these aims are from the beginning impossible or lacking in means.' But when, through the interplay of all the blind accidents which appear to dominate in unconscious nature, a general law of movement nevertheless imposes itself — only then does the question arise whether the thoughts and desires of consciously acting human beings are also dominated by such a law.

And the law is to be found, if one searches for it, through which the ideal driving forces of human beings are set into motion. A human being can only reach consciousness in a social relationship, thinking and acting with consciousness; the social grouping of which he is part awakens and directs his spiritual forces. The basis of all social community, however, is the form of production of material life, and this determining also in the last analysis the spiritual life process, in its manifold reflections. Historical materialism, far from denying the ideal forces, studies them down to their very basis, so that it can achieve the necessary clarity about where the power of ideas is drawn from. Human beings make their own history, certainly, but *how* they make history, this is dependent in each case upon how clear or unclear they are in their heads about the material connections between things. Ideas do not arise out of nothing, but are the product of the social process of production, and the more accurately an idea reflects this process, the more powerful it is. The human spirit does not stand *above*, but *within* the historical development of human society; it has grown out of, in and with material production. Only since this production has begun to develop out of a highly variegated bustle into simple and great contradictions, has it been able to recognize the whole relationship; and only after these latter contradictions have died or been overcome, will it win domination over social production, and will the 'prehistory of man come to an end' (Marx); and then 'men will make their own history with full consciousness, and the leap of man from the realm of necessity into that of freedom' will take place (Engels).[16]

For that reason, however, the previous development of society is not a dead mechanism in which man has served as a helpless pawn. The greater part of its total life each generation had to devote to the satisfaction of all its needs, the more dependent, that is, it remained upon nature, the smaller was the scope of its spiritual development. But this scope grew in the same measure as human beings acquired skills and accumulated experience, enabling them to dominate nature. The human mind acquired more and more mastery over the dead mechanism of nature, and the progressive development of the human race proceeded and proceeds through the mastery of man's mind over the process of production. 'The whole question of the domination of men over their environment' depended on their skill in producing their livelihood. 'Mankind are the only beings who may be said to have gained an absolute control over the production of food which at the outset they did not possess above other animals. . . .It is accordingly probable that the great epochs of human progress have been identified, more or less directly, with the enlargement of the sources of subsistence.'[17] If we follow Morgan's classification of human pre-history, then the first step from savagery is marked by the cultivation of articulated speech, the second by the use of fire, the third by the discovery of the bow and arrow, which already forms a very complex tool, and presupposes a long accumulated experience, and sharpened powers of the mind, that is a simultaneous knowledge of a whole number of other discoveries. On this latter stage of primitive man a certain control over production through the human mind is already to be found; wooden containers and tools, baskets plaited out of bark and reeds, sharpened stone tools and so on, were known.

According to Morgan, barbarism began with the introduction of pottery, which marks its lowest stage. The middle stage was brought in by the taming of livestock, the cultivation of plants for food and their irrigation, the use of stones and bricks in building. The highest stage of barbarism finally begins with the smelting of iron ore; at this stage the production of material life reaches an extraordinarily rich development; to it belong the Greeks of the age of Heroes, the Italian tribes shortly before the foundation of Rome, the Germans of Tacitus. This age saw the bellows, the clay oven, the smithy, the iron axe, the iron spade and sword, the copper-tipped spear, the embossed shield, the quern, the potter's wheel, the cart and the chariot, the building of ships with logs and beams, cities with stone walls and gables, with gates and towers, and marble temples. An attractive picture of the progress reached by the highest stage of barbarism is given us by the Homeric poems, which themselves are a classical witness to the spiritual life which grew out of these means of production. So humanity is not the helpless plaything of a dead mechanism, but its development consists precisely in the growing power of the human mind over the dead mechanism of nature. But — and this is only said by historical materialism — the human spirit develops from, with and out of the material mode of production. The human mind is not the father of the mode of production, but the mode of production is the mother of the human mind. And this relation appears with the most striking clarity in the prehistory of mankind.

The invention of the alphabet and its use for literary purposes marks the transition from barbarism to civilization. The written history of humanity begins, and in it the spiritual life appears to separate itself completely from its economic basis. But the appearance is deceptive. With civilization, with the dissolution of the gentile system, with the rise of the family, private property and the state, with the progressive division of labour, with the division of society into rulers and ruled, into oppressed and oppressor classes, the dependence of the spiritual on the economic development becomes infinitely less transparent and more complicated, but it does not end. The 'last reason by which the class differences are defended: that there must be a class which does not have to toil at the production of its daily means of living, so that it has time to take care of the spiritual work of society, has previously had its wider historical justification' (Engels) — previously, that is up to the industrial revolution of the last hundred years, which makes every ruling class a fetter on the development of the productive forces — but the division of society into classes grew solely out of economic development and thus the spiritual work of no class could separate itself from the economic basis to which it owed its origins. The depth of the fall from the simple moral heights of the old gentile society to the new society, which was dominated by the lowest interests, and was never anything other than the development of the small minority at the expense of the exploited and oppressed vast majority, was matched by the enormity of the spiritual development from the gens, which was still attached to the umbilical cord of natural social being, to modern society with its immense productive forces.[18]

As great as this progress was, as fine, precise and strong an instrument as the human mind became, being more and more able to bring nature irresistibly under control, its central motive forces still remained the economic struggle of different classes, the 'existing struggles between social productive forces, and productive relationships'; and so mankind only posed for itself such tasks as it could solve. Looked at more closely, as Marx explains, it will be found that the task only arises where the material conditions for its solution are already in existence, or at least in the process of becoming.

This connection is most easily recognized, when one traces back to their origins the great discoveries and inventions which have sprung from creative human minds — according to the ideological conception of both historical idealism and the materialism of the natural sciences — like Athena from the head of Zeus, and thus are supposed to have called forth the greatest economic upheavals. Each of these discoveries and inventions has a long pre-history.[19]

If one follows the individual stages of this pre-history, so one will discover everywhere the need which brought them about. There were good reasons why the origins of some of the most important discoveries, such as the discovery of gunpowder, and the art of book printing, which have 'changed the face of the earth', are shrouded in legend. They are not the work of individuals drawing inspiration from the mysterious depths of their genius. Even if individuals have greater responsibilities for them, it was only because these individuals recognized most sharply and deeply the economic necessity and the means for its satisfaction. It is not the discovery or the invention that caused the historical upheaval, but the social upheaval that brought about the discovery or the invention, and only when social upheaval has brought about a discovery or an invention does this become a world-shaking event. America had been discovered a long time before Columbus; already in the year 1,000, Normans had reached the North East coast of America, and had reached as far as the area of the present-day United States, but the discovered lands were quickly forgotten and lost from memory. Only when the beginning of capitalist development called forth the need for precious metals, new labour, and new markets, did the discovery of America mean an economic revolution. And it is well known that Columbus did not want to discover a new world out of the obscure urges of his genius, but was seeking the shortest way to the legendary treasures of the ancient culture of India.

On the day after the discovery of the first island, he wrote in his diary: 'These well-behaved people would make quite useful slaves' and his daily prayer went as follows: 'May the Lord in his mercy let me find the gold mines!' The 'Lord of Mercy' was the ideology of the time; today it is the admittedly much more hypocritical ideology of bringing 'humanity and civilization into the dark parts of the world.'

The proverbially sad fate of precisely the most inspired discoverer is not a proof of human ingratitude, as the ideological conception in its superficial manner asserts, but is rather an easily explained result of the fact that the discovery does not create the economic upheaval but rather the other way around. Sharp and farseeing minds recognize the task and its solution, where material conditions of its solution are still immature, and the existing social formation has not developed all the productive forces which are necessary for it. It is a notable fact, that precisely the discoveries which more than any previous ones have contributed towards extending human productive forces beyond all limits, have been fatal to the discoverers, and in fact disappeared more or less without a trace for centuries. In Danzig in 1529 Anton Müller discovered the so-called ribbon-loom (also called a small-wares loom), which produced from four to six pieces of cloth at the same time, but since the City Council was afraid that this discovery could make paupers of a large number of the workers, they suppressed it, and had the inventor secretly drowned or strangled. In Leyden the same machine was used in 1629, but the lacemakers' riots forced the authorities to ban it. In Germany, it was banned by Imperial Edicts in 1685 and in 1719. In Hamburg it was burned in public on the instructions of the magistrates. 'This machine, which shook Europe to its foundations, was in fact the precursor of the mule and the power loom, and of the industrial revolution of the 18th century.'[20] Hardly less tragic than the fate of Anton Müller was that of Denis Papin, who tried to construct a steam engine for industrial purposes while Professor of Mathematics in Marburg. Discouraged by the general opposition, he abandoned his machinery and built a steam boat in which he steamed off from Kassel to England down the Fulda in 1707. But in Münden the great wisdom of the authorities stopped his journey, and the Weser watermen smashed up the steam boat. Papin later died in England poor and deserted. Now it is clear that the discovery of the ribbon loom in the year 1529, by Anton Müller, or the discovery of the steam boat in 1707 by Denis Papin, were incomparably greater achievements of the human mind than James Hargreaves' invention of the jenny in 1764 and Fulton's invention of the steam boat in 1807. The fact that, despite this, the former failed and the latter was such a world-shaking success, is proof of the fact that economic development is the motive force for inventions and not vice-versa; that the human mind is not the originator but the executor of revolution in society.

Let us dwell for a moment on the invention of the art of printing and gunpowder, which have been the most exploited for strange mental gymnastics of historical idealism. As the trade in goods and the production of commodities developed in the Middle Ages, an infinite acceleration took place in the trade in ideas, which for its satisfaction required the mass production of literature. Thus it led to wood block prints, the production of books which were reproduced by printing off engraved plates. This so-called 'block' print had already increased so much at the beginning of the fifteenth century that it was the occasion for the formation of regular guilds, the most important of which were in Cologne, Augsburg, Nuremburg, Mainz and Lübeck. But the wooden block printers generally entered into a guild with the painters, not with the book-printers who followed, alongside whom they co-existed for a whole period for the reproduction of shorter writings. The printing of books did not arise out of letter printing, but out of metal handicrafts. It was a small step to cut up the wooden printing plates into separate letters and through any composition one desired to make the reproduction of books enormously quicker. But all these attempts failed through the technical impossibility of achieving even lines with wooden letter-types. The next step was to cut the letters in metal, but even this did not meet with any decisive success, both because the cutting of the metal types by hand required too much time, and because the unevenness of the letters was reduced but by no means ended. Both difficult conditions were solved only through the casting of metal type; and the use of hot lead is in fact the discovery of the art of book printing, the art of forming words, lines, sentences, and pages out of single moveable letters, and then their reproduction through printing. Gutenberg was a goldsmith, and so was Bernardo Gennini, who is said to have discovered the art of printing in Florence at the same time. The bitter and wearisome fight over the real discoverer of printing will never be decided, because everywhere that economic development posed the problem, the attempt to solve it was made with greater or less success. If one can assume that Gutenberg made the last, most decisive step with the greatest definitiveness and clarity, that is with the greatest success, so that the new art spread the quickest from Mainz, it was because he was the one who best understood how to draw the results of a host of experiences out of the partial or total failure of his predecessors. His contribution remains immortal, and his invention an admirable achievement of the human mind, but he planted no new root in the earth; rather he plucked a slowly ripened fruit.

The proverb that makes the invention of gunpowder the touchstone of human inventiveness is not so wrong after all; but it was precisely in relation to this discovery that the historical conceptions of both philosophical idealism and mechanical materialism suffered the most lamentable shipwrecks. Professor Kraus thinks that gunpowder did away with brute force and bondage, that it broke the power of the individual in favour of the general being, and that 'the immense majority of us' owe it to this invention that we all act and move as free men and not as bondsmen of the soil. And Professor Dubois-Reymond explains, in detail, that the Romans would have repelled all attacks from the Germani, from the Cimbri and the Teutones and even the Goths and Vandals with ease, if they had known about flintlocks. As usual, mechanical materialism goes even beyond philosophical idealism in its conceited schoolmaster's outlook. 'The backwardness of the ancients in science was disastrous for all mankind', writes Dubois-Reymond. 'This is one of the most important reasons for the failure of the old culture. The greatest misfortune which ever hit mankind, the invasion of the Mediterranean by the barbarians, probably could have been avoided, if the ancients had possessed the scientific knowledge we do today.' It is a pity M. Dubois-Reymond was not an ancient Roman, but then again perhaps it is as well. Because his very own philosophy of history proves that if, instead of being commander of the regiment of the Hohenzollerns' spiritual body-guards in the year 1870, he had been commander of a Roman legion at the time of the Punic wars, he would have been no more likely to have discovered gunpowder. In fact a bourgeois historian, Professor Delbrück, has opposed the fantastic hypothesis of Kraus and Dubois-Reymond. Delbrück is far from being a historical materialist, but he realizes that, for something to be invented, a continuous need has to be felt throughout several generations, indeed centuries; that one discovery is no more to be separated from the requirements of its time than a human being can be born without a mother; and that the assumption that any discovery could have been made at another time and caused another development of history is an empty fantasy game. In this respect, he has every right to consider his own conception scientific as opposed to the 'intellectual' games of Kraus and Dubois-Reymond. And he is especially right that the discovery, or rather the use of gunpowder, was not the cause but rather the lever of the fall of feudalism — moreover, a weak and basically non-essential lever; whether Delbrück goes too far in that direction in our opinion is not so important in this context.[21]

An economic upheaval brought about the dissolution of feudalism, and no part of the political superstructure of the material mode of production changes so clearly and quickly as the army. Bourgeois history has become quite clear about this, particularly as regards the Prussian military state. Gustav Freytag, who would like to spin out German history from the 'German soul', but who, through his special subject, the social life of ordinary people, is forced continually to admit historical materialism, writes as follows:

> The Frankish territorial forces of the Merovingians, the army of the age of lance-bearing knights, the Swiss and the hired lansquenets of the Reformation, the mercenaries of the Thirty Years War, were each the most characteristic formations of their time, growing out of the social conditions and changing with them. Thus the yeomanry of the landowners was rooted in the ancient order of parish and district; the huge armies of knights in the feudal order, and the hired lansquenets in the rise to prosperity of the burgesses, while the companies of travelling mercenaries were based on the growth of the territorial domination of the princes. They were followed by the standing armies of the despotic states of the eighteenth century with their trained mercenaries.[22]

The spear was only finally replaced by firearms in this 'standing army of trained mercenaries' in the days of Louis XIV and Prince Eugen, in an infantry which was more or less forcefully press-ganged out of the dregs of the nation, and which had to be held together by force. It was thus deprived of any aggressive initiative and could only be used as a shooting machine. Such a mercenary infantry was in every way the exact opposite of the yeomanry which had brought about the first decisive defeats of the feudal knights' armies in the fourteenth century at Morgarten and Sempach. This yeomanry fought with spears, and even with the most primitive weapons of the forest, such as catapults, but it drew its terrible striking power, which was unbeaten by the knights, from its old mark brotherhood principle, all for one and one for all.[23]

This simple contrast alone gives the lie to the assumption that the discovery of gunpowder caused the fall of feudalism. Feudalism fell through the growth of the cities, and the monarchy which was based on the cities.

The agricultural economy succumbed to the money and industrial economy, and so the feudal lords had to subordinate themselves to the cities and the princes. The new economic powers created the forms of war which corresponded to their economic forms; with their money they recruited armies from the proletariat, which were thrown onto the roads by the dissolution of feudalism; with their industry they made weapons, which were as superior to the feudal weapons as the capitalist form of production was to the feudal. Then they discovered — not gunpowder, since this reached Western Europe from the Arabs at the beginning of the fourteenth century — but gunpowder-firing. With firearms the superiority of the bourgeois over the feudal weapons was definitively established. The castle walls could no more withstand cannon balls than the armour of the knights could withstand musket bullets. But the art of shooting was not discovered in a day either. As always, here economic necessity was the mother of invention and the break-up of feudalism was so swift, the power of the towns, cities and princes grew so swiftly, that the inventive power of the human mind was not much aroused to improve the at first very awkward firearms, which were hardly an improvement over the crossbow and longbow. And why should it when the knights' armies were beaten even in places where they had superior firepower, as with Granson and Murten? And so the development of these weapons proceeded very slowly. We have already seen how late a suitable weapon was developed — with the flintlock — for the arming of the entire infantry. And this gun was possible only at a certain stage of capitalist development; it was the only weapon with which princely absolutism could fight out its trade wars on the basis of the standing army, with strategy and tactics dictated by the economic foundations. But if anyone were to lament the slow development of this spirit of discovery in previous centuries, then they should comfort themselves with a glance at our century, and derive the pleasing certainty that the human mind in reality is infinitely creative in the invention of lethal weapons, with economic development, in this case the uncontrolled movement of competition under monopoly capitalism, whipping it on, so to speak, from behind.

Historical materialism does not then claim that humanity is a helpless plaything of a dead mechanism; it does not deny the power of the idea. On the contrary, it is in agreement with Schiller, from whom the German cultural philistine chiefly draws his 'idealism', that the higher the human spirit develops,

> The more beautiful the riddles emerging from the night
> The richer is the world that it contains
> And broader streams the sea with which it flows
> And weaker yet the sightless power of fate.

Only historical materialism demonstrates the law of this development of thought, and finds the root of this law in that which first made man into man, the production and reproduction of immediate life. That beggarly pride which once decried Darwinism as the 'theory of the apes' may struggle against this, and find solace in the thought that the human spirit flickers like an unfathomable will-o'-the-wisp, and with Godlike creative powers fashions a new world out of nothing. This superstition was dealt with by Lessing, both in his mockery of the 'bald ability to act now in one way, now in another, under exactly the same circumstances', and also through his wise words:

> The pot of iron
> Likes to be lifted with silver tongs
> From the flame, the easier to think itself
> A pot of silver.

We can deal more briefly with the accusation that historical materialism denies all moral standards. It is certainly not the task of the history researcher to use moral standards. He should tell us how things were on the basis of an objective scientific investigation. We do not demand to know what he thinks about them according to his subjective moral outlook. 'Moral standards' are caught up, involved in a continuous transformation, and for the living generation to impose on former generations its changing standards of today, is like measuring the geological strata against the flying sand of the dunes. Schlosser, Gervinus and Ranke, and Janssen — each of them has a different moral standard, each has his own class morals, and even more faithfully than the times they depict, they reflect in their works the classes they speak for. And it goes without saying that it would be no different if a proletarian writer of history were to make rash criticisms of former times from the moral standpoint of his class today.

In this respect historical materialism denies all moral standards — but in this respect alone. It bans them from the *study of history* because they make all *scientific* study of history impossible.

But if the accusation means that historical materialism denies the role of moral driving forces in history, then let us repeat: the precise opposite is true. It does not deny them at all, but rather for the first time makes it possible to recognize them. In the 'material, scientifically determinable upheaval of the economic conditions of production' it has the only certain yardstick for investigating the sometimes slower, sometimes faster changes in moral outlook. These too are in the last analysis the product of the form of production, and thus Marx opposed the Nibelungen tales of Richard Wagner, who tried in the modern manner to make his love stories more piquant by means of a little incest, with the fitting words: 'In remote antiquity the sister was the wife and that was moral.' Just as thoroughly as it clears up the question of the great men who are supposed to have made history, historical materialism also deals with the images of historical characters that come and go in history according to their favour and disfavour in the eyes of different parties. It is able to do every historical personality justice, because it knows how to recognize the driving forces which have determined their deeds and omissions, and it can sketch in the fine shadings which cannot be attained by the coarser 'moral standards' of the ideological writing of history.

Take Kautsky's excellent writings on Thomas More. Thomas More is a real thorn in the flesh for the ideological historians. He was an early fighter for the bourgeois class, a well educated and free thinking man, learned humanist, and the first pioneer of modern socialism. But he was also the minister of a tyrannical prince, an opponent of Luther, and a persecutor of heretics; he was a martyr on behalf of the Papacy, and he is today a semi-official saint of the Catholic Church, and may yet be canonized. What can ideological writers of history do with a character such as this, whether they derive their 'moral standards' from Rome or Berlin? They can idealize him or run him down, or half idealize him, half run him down, but for all their 'moral yardsticks' they can never find the key to the historical understanding of the man. Kautsky, on the other hand, has performed this task brilliantly on behalf of historical materialism. He has shown that Thomas More was a whole man and that all the apparent contradictions of his character were indissolubly connected. There is infinitely more to be learned about the moral forces of the Reformation period from Kautsky's thin volume than from everything that Ranke wrote in five volumes or Janssen wrote in six thick ones, with their diametrically opposed 'moral standards' about the same period of history. That is why Kautsky's writings have been surrounded by a veil of silence. For this is what the 'moral standards' of the bourgeois historical science of today demand.

We have already mentioned that from the bourgeois side at least, one attempt has been made to make a scientific critique of historical materialism, and one more remark must be made about this attempt. It must be a limited one, however, since we do not want to waste time exposing point by point the twenty pages of distortions and misrepresentations of the materialist outlook on history lumped together by Herr Paul Barth.[24] His 'critical essay' is too insignificant for that — it is enough to draw from it some essential points, the explanation of which is useful for a positive understanding of historical materialism.

Herr Barth is first of all very disturbed about the fact that Marx formulates the materialist conception of history in 'an unfortunately very indeterminate way, patched together out of imagery, and only sometimes in his writings explaining and illustrating it with examples.' He recently aired his mental agonies on this account in an even more drastic form in a weekly magazine of the Bismarckian bourgeoisie, saying that the 'so-called materialist theory of history was a half-truth, that Karl Marx had spoken in a moment of journalistic frivolity, and unfortunately tried to back it with supposed "proof".' With the stern countenance of a judge, Herr Barth says that there are only three scientific writings by Marx, that is only three worthy of the attentions of a German professor, and these are *Capital*, *The Poverty of Philosophy*, and the precursor of *Capital*, *A Critique of Political Economy*. Everything else is 'popular' and does not concern Herr Barth. Equally, of Engels' writings he recognizes only *Anti-Duhring* and *Ludwig Feuerbach* as worthy of his attention. Herr Barth follows the opposite principle with Kautsky, whom he only knows as the 'author of an essay' in *Neue Zeit*, the popular organ of the Marxists, 'which has caused great harm' through the spreading of 'Marxist folly'; of Kautsky's 'only scientific writings', such as the book on More, Herr Barth knows nothing or wants to know nothing. Why he makes all these profound distinctions will soon become clear.

In the first place Herr Barth wants to prove that there is no 'primacy of economics over politics'. Marx is said to speak in *Capital* about common, direct social labour in a natural form, which is to be found in the historical threshold of all cultures, of immediate ruling and slave relations at the beginning of history. The word 'direct', of which there is not even the slightest mention in Marx, is elucidated thus by Herr Barth: 'That is to say, as with Hegel, incapable of closer description.' He adds triumphantly that Marx did not explain the transition from the natural forms of labour to the relation between the masters and slaves either. Now Marx did not have the slightest occasion to make such an explanation in the section of *Capital* where he touches upon this development, but he intended to give it, in connection with the research of Morgan, in a special essay, which as death prevented him from carrying out his intention was then published by Engels, becoming known to the public more than half a century before Herr Barth proceeded to the smashing of historical materialism. In Engels' work on *The Origin of the Family*, etc., the economic development of the classes from gentile society — the economic transition from immediate socialized labour to master and slave relationships — is set out; but, and here the real meaning of these distinctions becomes clear, Engels' work is not only 'scientific' but also 'popular' and Herr Barth nowhere mentions it. And then he begins to 'explain'. Where Marx explains the master and slave relationships 'incapable of closer description' at the beginning of society, Herr Barth writes: 'Since at that time no private property in land or capital existed, and thus no opportunity for subjugation through economic means, thus only political causes can remain for this original enslavement — war and the taking of prisoners of war.' Although Herr Barth cannot avoid asking if these features of war did not have an economic basis, and replies: 'For the most part, but not exclusively', 'according to the writings of the anthropologists,' the wars of the savages were caused by religious motives, chieftains' ambitions, and revenge, that is, 'ideological causes'. But instead of at least examining, first of all, what value this evidence of the anthropologists has, and secondly if there are not economic driving forces to be found disguised by 'the ideological root causes', Herr Barth only makes the stupefying revelation, in passing, that the conquest of Asia by Alexander is to be attributed to the 'ambition' of the Macedonian king, and the expansionist drive of Islam was due to 'religious enthusiasm' and then reaches the triumphant conclusion that slavery in both history and prehistory was 'to a large degree, and in the last instance, a political product', and that 'thus politics are shown to determine economics in the deepest and most complete way'. Upon which Herr Barth then, with the utmost perspicacity, but not without the help of Rodbertus, proves that slavery is a 'powerful economic category'.

In this way Herr Barth skirts round the scientific proof of historical materialism, which as we have seen in no way denies the presence of ideal motive forces, such as ambition, revenge or religious fervour, but only claims that these motive forces are determined in the last analysis through other, economic, motive forces. And insofar as Herr Barth even considers bringing a proof, a single proof for his claims, the materialist conception of history immediately comes into its own. As the only evidence of the thirst for revenge as a motive for wars between savages he adduces the English anthropologist Taylor, who also discusses the not unknown fact of blood revenge among barbarian tribes. If Herr Barth had not excluded Engels' work *The Origin of the Family* from his consideration as being too 'popular', he would quickly have discovered that blood revenge is also part of the 'legal superstructure' of gentile society, just as the death penalty is part of the legal superstructure of civilized society. Engels says of gentile society:

> Argument and strife are decided by the society of those concerned, be it the gens or the tribe or the individual gentes among themselves — blood revenge, of which our death penalty is only the civilized form, embodying all the advantages and disadvantages of civilization, threatens only as an extreme, rarely used remedy.

According to the conditions of production of gentile society, what was outside the tribe was also outside the law, and when Taylor says that the exaction of revenge usually degenerated into open war when the murderer belonged to another tribe, and such a blood feud would cause bitter wars for generations, then Herr Barth will see that the 'thirst for revenge', which causes the wars of savages, has no ideological cause, but is a form of justice flowing from a specific form of economy. Of course the barbaric penal code, like that of civilization — as with the anti-socialist laws — can be misused, and is indeed misused where barbaric tribes come into contact with civilization and degenerate through its influence, but in that case the development really is from an ideological to an economic category, to the thirst not for *revenge* but for *robbery*. To contrast Herr Barth's English researcher with the Frenchman Dumont, we find Dumont writing about the Albanese, ancient Europeans and for the most part Christians — who 'attacked the neighbouring tribes, *especially when they were of another religion*, and stole their livestock, a sport which promised good profits in peace-time. Reasons for the attacks were not even necessary: the stranger was the natural enemy and should keep a good watch; he who failed to keep a good watch and allowed himself to be attacked was the guilty party. Especially between people of different tribes differences arose from the tiniest reasons. Insults open up the struggle, and as soon as blood is shed, the whole tribe declares its solidarity with the family of the victim. Blood revenge still persists in mountainous regions.' With this Herr Barth has a sample of the 'religious motives' in the wars of the barbarians, and perhaps he may have some inkling of how 'good profits' could awaken the 'ambitious intentions of a chieftain'. On these two points he does not refer to any 'anthropologists', but escapes with a sudden leap into 'historical times', when the 'ambition' of Alexander of Macedonia and the 'religious wars of Islam' are supposed to be 'as clear as daylight'. 'As clear as daylight' they are indeed, Herr Barth, for the crude conceptions of bourgeois historical research, caught up in the outer surface of things. Or perhaps not, for Alexander's German biographer, the Prussian historian Droysen, does not start his book with Barth's position, 'Alexander's ambition created a new period in world history', but with his own much more judicious remark, 'the *name* Alexander *marks* the end of one world epoch and the start of a new one.' Alexander's ambition may be clear as daylight, but what lies below the light of day is the real question, and Herr Barth carefully avoids this question.

Immediately following his borrowing from Rodbertus about the important economic role of slavery in history, he continues: 'In talking about the ending of the Middle Ages Marx puts forward material which destroys his own arguments, in which the dispersal of the tenants by the feudal lords, who transformed the land into sheep runs with a few shepherds because of the rising profits from grazing, the practice of enclosure, and the transformation of those peasants into free proletarians, who now placed themselves at the disposal of the up-and-coming industries, formed one of the first causes of the original "accumulation" of capital. This agricultural revolution, according to Marx, goes back to the rise of wool manufacture, but according to his own explanation, the feudal powers, the greedy landlords, become its most powerful levers, that is a political power becomes a link in the chain of economic development.' And that is the end of it. Now we know, according to the point of view of certain learned men, Marx is literally drugged with 'arguments against himself', but how and where he argues against himself in the points raised by Herr Barth is beyond our modest powers of understanding. Herr Barth's proof could perhaps achieve a superficial brilliance in appearance had the landowners 'used the lever of legislation' in order to expropriate the peasants — but it is only a superficial appearance, because even then the politics would of course depend on the economics. But when one looks up the reference in Marx, it emerges that the legislature actually attempted weakly to oppose the economic upheaval, and failed because of the needs of the beginning of the era of capitalist production, in which the great feudal lords, 'in defiant opposition to King and Parliament' chased the peasants from their land, and usurped their common lands. The 'self-contradiction' in Marx thus lies in the fact that Herr Barth, with his magic formula, 'therefore', transforms the 'feudal powers, the greedy landlords' into a 'political power'. In this case indeed, the speed of the hand deceives the eye.

Immediately after the statements quoted, Herr Barth 'goes even further back' and seeks to prove that the feudal forces arose thanks to 'political factors'. We can overlook this, on the one hand because Herr Barth does not polemicize any further against Marx and Engels, but adduces a completely inadequate proof from various bourgeois authorities, wrapped up in all kinds of sophism and phrasemongering; and on the other hand because the social origins of feudalism can be grasped, so to speak, with both hands, and have been shown convincingly recently even by the more important bourgeois historians.[25] For the modern period Herr Barth attempts to prove the dependence of economics on politics by saying that, in the era of discoveries, trade followed upon the lust for conquest, that is upon expeditions which were undertaken for political motives. In a previous section we have already seen, however, what connection there is between economics and discoveries and inventions in history, and we do not have to go into the theory of the 'lust for conquest' of Columbus, and so on. Trade did not *follow* the discoveries, but on the contrary *led to* them; here too, the economics were the basic factor. And when, finally, Herr Barth refers to the very close connection between the absolute monarchy as a state form and the great number of monopolies that were only possible under such a monarchy, he should have known in advance from Luther's complaints about the 'monopoly companies' (*Gesellschaften Monopolia*)[26] that the monopolies existed long before the absolute monarchy, and that the 'close connection' was not just created by the monopolies as an economic form of absolute monarchy, but by absolute monarchy as a political form of the capitalist mode of production.

And with these five crushing blows Herr Barth thinks he has laid flat historical materialism, insofar as it makes politics dependent on economics.

Herr Barth wants to go on to dismiss the view held by Marx that property relations are the legal expression of relations of production; that, as Herr Barth expresses it, law is 'a mere function of economics'. 'At first glance this appears to be false, since the same relations of production can be seen under very different legal forms, as Marx himself quotes communist agriculture without slavery and agriculture with private ownership and slavery, that is, two different legal forms for the same stage of production.' Is this really to be believed? Having once heard tell that agriculture is a *branch* of production, Herr Barth thinks it is also a production *relation,* and a *stage* in production! In Marx's view, the ownership of land and changes in its ownership arise out of the production *relations* in agriculture. According to whether it is carried out in common or privately, each of which can develop and have developed at the most various *stages* of production, there arise the most varied degrees of common and private ownership. 'At first glance this appears to be right', but for Herr Barth, it is all the same: member of the gens and Roman latifundist, member of the mark[27] and feudal lord, farmer, junker and bondsmen, they are all part of the agricultural *branch* of production, and so exist in the same production *relation* and at the same *stage* of production, and happen by chance to lead differing lives only by virtue of that law which leads an independent existence and falls like snow, heaven knows whence.

In the meantime, 'skipping over more distant examples', as Herr Barth puts it, 'we can still see today how certain ideas of law and political principles, which work against the free operation of the economic forces, first in Britain, then in almost every civilized country, have created legislation for the protection of workers and are continually struggling to extend it.' With this sentence, Herr Barth announces that he has not even understood historical materialism in the most superficial sense, if he sees the most platitudinous slogans of Manchesterism as its quintessence. In fact, he knows from Marx's *Capital* that the English factory acts were the result of an extremely long and hard class struggle between the aristocracy, bourgeoisie and proletariat; they had therefore an economic, not a moral or political root. And as far as the 'other civilized countries' are concerned, Herr Barth should be well aware, if only from his own dear fatherland, what little effect 'legal conceptions and political principles' have on 'economic forces'. The salubrious effects of the English Factory Acts had been displayed to the whole world for two decades when the North German Diet discussed the Statute of Trades (*Gewerbeordnung*) in 1869, and if that enlightened body really was ignorant of English conditions, the few Social Democratic deputies took care to draw their attention to the 'legal conceptions and political principles' of the English Factory Acts. Did the North German Diet then consider the demand that legal protection of labour, however modest, should be included in the Statute of Trades? It never occurred to them. And why not? Let Herr Barth learn from the Official Historiographer of the Prussian State: 'It can be clearly recognized from certain paragraphs of the Statute of Trades that the employers were strongly represented in the Diet.'[28] That is putting it mildly, and even then Treitschke makes convulsive efforts to defend the North German Diet against the charge of class self-interest. But this involuntary testimony is enough to explode all the chatter about the 'legal conceptions and political principles' that are supposed to have fathered the legal protection of labour. Whatever has been achieved in Germany up to now in the way of such protection is due entirely to the struggle of the German working class, as Bismarck admits, involuntarily again, but all the more convincingly for that. Meanwhile Herr Barth has had an opportunity to study the other side of the coin in the Imperial Decrees of February 1890. They too, let it be said, proceeded from 'certain legal concepts and political principles', and moreover the 'political power' with all its forces stood behind them, but nevertheless their effect was zero because the 'economic forces' were opposed to them.

'The Marxists', Herr Barth further states, 'are as quick to dismiss morals as merely phenomena associated with economics, in a certain sense as a by-product of economics, as they are politics, and just as incorrectly.' Notice how Barth speculates on the 'moral indignation' of the philistine by a spiteful distortion of what 'Marxists' have to say about the reflection in moral attitudes of the struggles of economic development. For his own part he thinks that moral conceptions receive a 'supernatural, metaphysical sanction' from religion, and that from this connection they gain an existence that is as independent as that of religions, acting and reacting by their own inner energy. Religion, he says, stands far away from economics through its origins:

it is not to be excluded that economics has an effect upon it, but this is only claimed by Marx and not proved. As opposed to this, what can be grasped easily in history is the opposite to what Marx claimed, that is a deep influence of religion on economics. 'In the East, through religion, a specially privileged priesthood was formed, freed from physical work, through the tributary obligations of the other classes, and selected for spiritual activity; that is the use of a part of the product of the economy was determined through religion. While in the Graeco-Roman culture, priestly activity was seldom incumbent upon special organs, Christianity went back to the oriental differentiation, created a separate priesthood, which it richly endowed, and thus set aside a part of the economic goods as a material substrate for religious activity, which soon became general intellectual activity.' This is Herr Barth word for word, and here again we must follow him step by step for a little while.

It appears that he has never asked himself the question where the 'differentiation' came from in the 'orient', and why Christianity went back to it. And it is all the more remarkable, since he claims to know Marx's *Capital*, and has therefore also read the sentence: 'The necessity for predicting the rise and fall of the Nile created Egyptian astronomy and with it the dominion of the priests, as directors of agriculture.'[29] And the same role which the Nile played for the Egyptians was played by the Tigris and the Euphrates, the Yang-tse and the Hoang-Ho for other oriental civilizations. The Russian scientist Mechnikov said concerning this that 'such a food-provider of a river demands on pain of death, a close and lasting solidarity between sections of the population who are often hostile and even enemies; it sentences everyone to the same work, the use of which is only shown by time, and the plan of which often remains incomprehensible to ordinary people. This is the real cause of the awe and deification of the river as a god who succours and decrees, kills and gives life; who trusts his secrets only to a select few, and from ordinary mortals demands blind obedience.'[30] Thus in the East an especially privileged profession of priests was created through the economy, and not, as Herr Barth claims, through religion; religion did not determine economics, but on the contrary, economics determined religion.

Why did Christianity go back to this 'oriental differentiation'? Why did it create a caste of priests who owned one third of the land, half the income and two-thirds of the wealth of the whole of Europe, as Herr Barth says with astonishment? Yes, if Herr Barth had not excluded the scientific works of Kautsky from his 'scientific critique', then he would not betray his lack of knowledge in such a pitiful fashion.

> When the Germanic tribes invaded the Roman empire, the Church represented against them the heirs of the Caesars, the organization which held the state together, the representatives of the mode of production belonging to the end of the imperial epoch. Pitiable as this state was, degenerate as the form of production was, both of them were far superior to the economic and political conditions of the barbaric Germans ...The Church taught them higher forms of agriculture; the monasteries remained model agricultural institutions until late in the Middle Ages. It was also the clergy who brought art and craft skills to the Germans; not only did the peasant prosper under the protection of the Church, it also sheltered the larger part of the cities until they were strong enough to defend themselves. Trade was especially favoured by it. The big markets were mostly held next to or inside the churches. The church was the only power which in the Middle Ages took care of the maintenance of the main trade roads, and made travelling easier through the hospitality of the monasteries. Some of these, such as the Hospices on the Alpine passes, served almost exclusively for the encouragement of the movement of trade ...And the fact that the whole knowledge of the Middle Ages was to be found exclusively in the Church alone, that it produced the master-builders, the engineers, doctors, historians and diplomats is well known. The whole material life of people, and with it their spiritual life, emanated from the Church ...it made the Germanic chieftain, the democratic leader of the people and the commander-in-chief, into a monarch; but with the power of the monarch over the people, the power of the Church over the monarch also grew. He became its puppet, the Church changed from a teacher to a ruler.'[31]

And so the Church used its all-embracing position of power to accumulate colossal wealth, as Herr Barth can read in detail in Kautsky. He will then immediately grasp that, as he puts it, 'Christianity', though he ought logically to say, the feudal mode of production, 'selected a part of the economic goods' as the 'material substrate', not for 'religious activity', but for the direction of economic production. The more superfluous this direction became through the rise of the bourgeois mode of production, the more the economic wealth of the Church was seized wholesale. According to ideological conceptions, Protestantism is the renewal of primitive Christianity, of religious feeling and inner belief, and in a certain sense this is also true: the economic upheavals of the Reformation period threw the masses, especially in Germany, into such an abyss of distress that they preferred to forget their earthly condition, and to concern themselves more intensively with God and the Devil, with heavenly bliss and infernal torture, than the carefree Catholicism of the Middle Ages, with its love for life, ever did. If Herr Barth were right, the religious activity of the priests of this form of Christianity would have to have received an even richer 'material substrate', but the proverbial poverty of the pastor of the Protestant Church must make him think otherwise on this count.

We shall skip over Herr Barth's two sentences about the religious origin of the Crusades, since this question has already been explained at length by Kautsky. But his trump card, with which he tries to prove 'the determining importance of religion for the whole life process in the clearest way', must be looked at more closely. He considers this proof irrefutable 'when two peoples, the same in everything but religion, show a completely different development in their conditions and achievements'. He proposes the Ottomans and Magyars as two such peoples, being closely related; they were neighbours in their original homes in the Turanic basin, the former moving towards Europe at the end of the ninth century, the latter in the twelfth century. For two hundred years, the Ottomans were far more advanced than the Magyars; but then the irresistible decline of the Ottomans began, while the Magyars remain a nation with a future, developing economically and politically. 'Since the remaining factors are more favourable for the Ottomans than the Magyars, only the difference between their religious can explain any divergence. Christianity, ascribing a higher value to spiritual powers, drove the Magyars to a higher spiritual development, while Islam, having less spiritual content, made the Ottomans less capable of competition with the Christian peoples.' We will gladly spare Herr Barth a refutation of all the secondary nonsense that is hidden in these few sentences, for example the superb imputation that derives the inextricable confusion of Germans, Jews, Slavs, Rumanians, Magyars and above all mixed races, which populates Hungary, as a pure-blooded race from the Turanic basin. It would take us too far to investigate here where the mass of the people is more 'degenerate' spiritually and morally, in Hungary or in Turkey, although we could refer to the fact that Marx, who has studied these things a little more clearly than Herr Barth, writing to Liebknecht, characterizes the Turkish peasantry — the mass of the Turkish population — as 'unquestionably one of the most hard-working and moral representatives of the peasantry in Europe.'[32] In order to smash Herr Barth's whole proof, it is enough to point out the world historical fact, which I hope is not unknown to Herr Barth, that throughout the whole of the Middle Ages Islamic culture ranked far above Christian culture. Of the three great areas of culture which inherited the Roman-Hellenic culture, the Roman-German, the Greek-Slav, and the Egyptian-Syrian, Arab culture, the latter took over the whole of the knowledge of antiquity in the fields of mathematics, astronomy, chemistry, mechanics and medicine; it was not Rome and not Constantinople but Alexandria which was the centre of science in the Roman Empire. Now the religious expression of the Germanic-Roman sphere of culture was the Roman Church, and that of the Greek-Slav sphere was the Greek Church, but that of the Arab Egyptian-Syrian sphere was Islam. And if Herr Barth's famous proof is true, then it would hold good for the whole of the Middle Ages, that 'Islam, ascribing a greater value to spiritual forces, drove the Arabs to a higher spiritual development while Christianity, having less spiritual content, made the Roman-Germanic peoples less capable of competing with the Mohammedans.' But of course, Herr Barth is treading on shaky ground: it is not religion but economics which determines the whole life process, and because Islamic culture did not outgrow its economic cell, the original village community, which still exists in the East today, therefore it was transcended by the Christian culture, which developed out of the feudal into the bourgeois mode of production, of course not *because of* but *despite* the Christian Church, which itself became a mere victim of this development irresistibly bleeding to death. Marx correctly says that every history of religion that sees it independently from its material base is uncritical: that it is in fact much easier to find the earthly nub of the misty religious images through analysis than to develop the glorified form out of the ordinary real circumstances of life. But this is the only materialist and therefore scientific method. And following this method, the most important phases of Christianity have been examined in order to reveal everywhere the dependence of religious conceptions on the relevant, immediate process of production.[33]

The spiritual power of Christianity, as an independent creative and effective factor, thus disappears without trace. The old heathen natural and popular religions, as long as there was no natural science, provided an understanding of nature for men producing under simple and transparent relationships. Christianity, by contrast, had a purely economic origin; it was a social, a world, a mass religion, which arose *on the basis* of the Roman empire, and *out of* different ideologies of its different peoples under the impact on the mind and mood of the people of the sinister and mysterious process of the economic collapse. With every upheaval of the mode of production, the spiritual content of the Christian religion changed with varying rapidity. This has become clear even to the better bourgeois historians, such as Gustav Freytag, who emphasizes that the Christian faith had already made great changes in the first century of its existence. It continually succumbed to these changes following the changes in economic development. If one wanted to determine a spiritual content of Christianity common throughout all the changes in time, then one would have at the most a few lifeless formulae at hand, and scarcely that — formulae which at their best could not move a feather, let alone a world. As the world religion of a world empire, Christianity had to develop an unusual adaptability to the most varying economic conditions, and to their ideological requirements; in Italy, it took over many components of the mythology of antiquity, in Germany it took over equally strong components of the Germanic religions, in China the veneration of Confucius and the cult of ancestors. And if the Bible was the book of books for the European peoples for more than a thousand years, if it had an extraordinarily lasting effect on the spiritual and religious conceptions of these people, then this did not take place because of its godly and unchallengeable truth, but precisely because of its countless contradictions. Kautsky said of it succinctly: 'This book consists of the spiritual condensation of the most varied social conditions and tendencies from the barbarian gentile society to the society of the Roman Empire, which had reached the peak of simple commodity production, and had collapsed on the threshold of capitalist production. Up to the time of the rule of the capitalist mode of production, there was no class, no party, which could not find prototypes and arguments in the Bible.' The more capitalist society develops however the more the spiritual influence of the Bible decreases, the more transparent becomes the economic process of production, the more the religious reflection of the real world becomes extinguished, and finally, the 'form of the social process of life, that is the material process of production is deprived of its veils of mystery, once production comes under the conscious planned control of free social human beings.' (Marx) It was precisely in its medieval heyday that the Catholic Church most clearly appeared as the political organization of a definite socio-economic formation. Herr Barth could also have consulted Kautsky to learn something about this, before having the, to put it mildly, remarkable naivety of deriving the Saxon wars of Charlemagne, and the wars against the Wends of the later Saxon Emperors, from 'religious motives'. The most 'religious' of these emperors was Heinrich II, who was even sanctified by the Roman Church. In Heinrich's own time, at the beginning of the eleventh century, lived an even more fiery evangelizer of heathens in the form of the Polish King Boleslav. Boleslav was severely oppressing the heathen Liutians who lived on this side of the Oder in what is now Mark Brandenburg, and who twenty years before had thrown off the yoke of the Christian Germans in a terrible uprising. According to Herr Barth's fine theory of history, the holy Heinrich should have sung an ambrosian song of praise that the heathen idol-worshippers were finally to be converted by a fellow Christian prince. Instead of this, Heinrich made a pact *with* the Liutians, *against* the Polish king. The Liutians agreed to observe certain Christian festivals in their country, and promised that they would pay him tribute if he would grant all their communities the ordering of their own affairs and the free practice of their heathen religion. Then together, the Liutians with their pagan images in the vanguard, they attacked the Polish king.[34]

The extension of Christianity was in those days the ideological clothing for the extension of state power; the foundation of a bishopric in a heathen land meant its incorporation in the state which had formed the bishopric — meant the exploitation, subjugation and enslavement of the defeated people through the Roman form of production. And a holy king would rather refrain from all Christian articles of faith and reconcile himself with all the horrors of heathendom than allow an equally holy king to have so much as one little lump of the soil of the country over which he thought he had the holy right of conquest. But what must this 'lofty cultural mission' of Christianity have looked like to these poor rogues of Liutians, who only bought themselves a short reprieve from the gallows by playing one hungry wolf off against another! Just over one hundred years later, another Polish Boleslav attacked the heathen Pomeranians for 'religious motives'. He laid waste the country; whole areas of land were totally devastated and the inhabitants fled across the sea or hid themselves in the forests. When Stettin was finally conquered, the people who were still there gave themselves up and promised what the plunderers had demanded first of all — the acceptance of Christianity, in other words subjugation to Polish rule. But this brought difficulties of its own.

Boleslav had hardly marched off and sent Bishop Bernhard as his evangelist, when the Pomeranians made short shrift of this devout man of God, driving him back home so that he was lucky to get away with his life. Incidentally, it is a fairy tale spread by ideological historians that the ill-treatment and murders so often carried out by the heathen peoples on the Christian missionaries of the Middle Ages derived from their bloodthirsty fanaticism. The old natural and folk religions were usually tolerant, simply because they reflected a good-natured spiritual relationship between man and nature, and believers did not care how other people tried to explain this relationship. By contrast, social world-religions are usually intolerant simply because, as Marx says, under their ideological cover they bring into conflict the 'most violent, petty and hateful passions in the human breast, the furies of private interest'. If despite this the medieval heathens killed the Christian missionaries so frequently (and except for a few upright ideologists they were not the best specimens), they acted with the same tragic short-sightedness as did workers who went machine-breaking at the time machines were first introduced. The missionaries were certainly the bearers of a higher mode of production, but it could not be expected that the heathens, for whom this mode of production represented the most atrocious exploitation and repression, would understand the 'higher point of view'. They thought they could smash the thing itself by destroying those who were its bearers.

Bishop Bernhard therefore returned defeated to Gnesen, and told Duke Boleslav, poor and helpless preacher of the gospel that he was, he had achieved nothing; that the Duke must send a splendid, rich prince of the Church to impress these vile heathens, or in other words that he must try to achieve with money what it had proved impossible to achieve with arms. As we know, the Duke tried to get Bishop Otto of Bamberg for this missionary work. He had proved himself a skilful and quick-witted diplomat in the struggles between the Emperor and the Pope; richly laden with presents, surrounded by a huge following, he moved into Pomerania, and by bribing heathen chieftains met with some success. But in Stettin the mass of the people opposed him completely. They allowed the Bishop to preach in peace, but before submitting to baptism demanded a sizeable reduction in the money tax and war dues imposed on them by the Duke, and only after lengthy negotiations, after messengers had been sent to Gnesen and the Duke's agreement to the demands for lessening the burdens had been delivered in writing, did Otto obtain his aim. The people of Stettin allowed themselves to be baptized and even destroyed the pagan temples, but pocketed the treasures for themselves, after the Bishop, supposedly out of generosity, had refused them. He moved off with an empty purse, but with the fame of being the apostle of Pomerania, a title he still enjoys today, since according to the reliable statements of the ideological historians, the 22,166 Pomeranians who had been so hastily baptized by Otto were converted to the belief in the holy trinity by his impressive rhetoric.

These examples certainly show the meaning of the 'religious motives' of the medieval conversion of the Slavs; they could be multiplied a hundred times, but we can dwell upon them no longer. Just as little can we dwell upon the economic basis of the recent history of religion, which was clarified by Engels, Kautsky and others a considerable time ago. What does need clarifying is the one objection Herr Barth makes to the materialist conception of the Reformation period. In an essay in *Neue Zeit* it was fittingly remarked that all the reformations and all the wars fought under the related religious banners from the thirteenth to the seventeenth century, were from the theoretical point of view nothing other than the repeated attempts of the bourgeoisie, the city plebeians, and those peasants who had become rebellious with them, to adapt the old theological conception of the world to the changed economic conditions and the situation in life of the new class. This 'lowering' is opposed by Herr Barth with the profound words, 'for the sake of this the Lombardic cities are ignored, though they were the most advanced in trade and did not have to make this adaptation to Catholicism of their thoroughly new way of life, but quietly kept their old forms of religion.'[35]

Since Herr Barth teaches logic, he really ought to know the saying: 'All city burgesses carried out reformations' is quite different from saying: 'all reformations started with the city burgesses.' And if he does not know this, then it would be as well for him not to get infected with 'Marxist impatience' and accuse honest people without further ado of scientific forgery. Moreover, his ingenious objection had been disproved two years earlier, before it even came to light, namely by Kautsky in *Thomas More* as follows: 'The more the production of commodities developed, the more national sentiment was strengthened, the more papal the Italians became. The rule of the Papacy meant the domination and exploitation of Christianity by Italy.' Once more Herr Barth's fine tactics are to be admired; the advantages he derives from taking notice only of the 'scientific' and not of the 'popular' works of Marx and Engels are matched by the advantages he derives from knowing only Kautsky's 'popular' works and not his 'scientific' ones.

But Herr Barth reaches his highest stature, when he is fighting for his own hearth and home. Philosophy is supposed in the last analysis to rest upon an economic basis? Horror of horrors! 'It has,' thunders Herr Barth, 'its origins and progress in a special, spiritually highly developed class, which although it is still closely related to the life of the people in its origins, and especially in its religious life, soon creates its own life, ruled by an esoteric tradition and comes to follow its own laws, more and more independently of the life of the people, but without losing its capacity for an effect upon the life of the people.' Should we disturb Herr Barth's illusions, that from Heraclitus to Paul Barth a chain of mysterious beings float over humanity, following their own laws, and occasionally giving the people a philosophical jab in the ribs from on high? It would be too cruel. But sadly, Herr Barth himself descends to our poor earth and tells us: 'Rousseau lived in a society of the most excessive class differences and privileges, and subordination to an all-powerful despotism, but through the method inherited from antiquity and continued by Hobbes and Locke, of the rational construction of the state, Rousseau came to the idea of a kind of society which was founded on general equality and the sovereignty of the people, which was in diametrical opposition to the constitution of France at the time. His theory became practice through the Convention, so that philosophy determined politics and indirectly also economics.' We dip the flag in the face of this philosophical philosophy of history. Rousseau was not the spokesman of the bourgeois class, which through its economic development blew up the absolutist feudal state, but rather the bourgeois classes were the obedient pupils of the schoolmaster Rousseau who made the French Revolution on his instructions by following the ancient recipe. We gladly admit that the bourgeois writing of history is on the whole no longer capable of such charming jokes.

Herr Barth's friendly advice, however, to take to heart the concluding words of Albert Lange's *History of Materialism*, we must decline with thanks. Lange does not come anywhere near historical materialism in a single word he says; what has to be said from the standpoint of materialism about Lange's work — which is excellent in many respects, but in no way defensible throughout — has already been said by the worker-philosopher, Joseph Dietzgen, whom Engels credited with re-discovering materialist dialectics independently of Marx and even of Hegel. For our part, we recommend that Herr Barth reads the work of this simple tanner, and when he has spiritually digested it, he should start his academic philosophizing anew from the very beginning.[36]

Herr Barth's last Parthian shot is his claim that Marx's theory of history is called materialist, despite the fact that certain material elements such as climate and race are completely neglected by it. In very deed! Look at the following statement by Marx: 'Apart from the degree of development, greater or less, in the form of social production, the productiveness of labour is fettered by physical conditions. These are referable to the constitution of man himself (race, etc.) and to surrounding nature. The external physical conditions fall into two great economic classes, (1) Natural wealth in means of subsistence, i.e., a fruitful soil, waters teeming with fish, etc., and (2) natural wealth in the instruments of labour, such as waterfalls, navigable rivers, wood, metal, coal etc. At the dawn of civilization, it is the first class that turns the scale: at a higher stage of development, it is the second' (*Capital* Vol. 1, p. 512). But it is really not worth speaking out against the shadow-boxing of Herr Barth in a serious way. When historical materialism says that man does not only live in nature, but also in society, it does not say what Herr Barth means to say with his chatter of climate and race: man lives only in society but not in nature.

All the same, Herr Barth has touched upon a problem which has caused much confusion in bourgeois minds, and therefore merits being explained somewhat more clearly. Historical materialism sees historical development in the gradual progression from the domination of man by nature to the domination of nature by man.

This progress is one and the same as the progress of countless tribes of men, who developed out of the animal world to the one social community, which some day will encompass the whole of the human race. The course of history is not the 'differentiation of the homogenous, but the assimilation of the heterogeneous'.[37] That differentiation was the legendary conception, as it is found in the Biblical genealogical construction of Ham, Shem and Japhet, in Tacitus' German genealogy of the three brothers Ingaev, Istaev and Hermin, or the Slav Czech, Lech and Russ. This assimilation, however, is a scientific conception derived as much from what daily takes place before our eyes, as it is from the investigations into the history of primitive man.

It is one of the insoluble contradictions in which mechanical materialism moves in the field of history, that it totally denies in the struggle for existence in human society the principle of evolution with which, in the realm of nature, it explains the peculiarities of a given species as the adaptation to their environment in the fight for existence, and claims that the human race here has certain permanent features which it has never had and never will have. In tortured additions to this indefensible conception, in the effort to make it compatible with clearly contradictory facts, the concept of race has become so indeterminate, that Gumplowicz says correctly: 'Here everything is arbitrary and subjective appearance and opinion: nowhere a firm ground, nowhere a certain starting point or point of reference and also nowhere a positive result.' In fact already in the pre-historical primitive times, the crossing and mixture of different races and tribes had begun, and the first civilizations of antiquity are proved by the Russian researcher Mechnikov to have been the result of a very colourful mixture of different races and tribes, of combinations in which the relative importance of the different combinations had never been remotely understood. Thus for example, it is difficult to weigh which of the three races, the black, the white or the yellow did the most for the civilization of ancient Egypt. The history of Chaldaea even shows that the black race, the so-called Kushites, were more advanced than any of the others in civilization. It advances us even less to take language instead of blood or colour as the sign of differentiation between races. In each of the main language groups, the Aryan, Semitic and Mongolian, there are people of the most varied origins, and if Herr Barth does have some reservations about the utterances of some 'brilliant' statesman or other, to the effect that 'race is everything' and yet claims that race is important, and tries to support this claim by insisting that the Aryan race is superior to the Semitic in its 'political abilities', then we must say in this connection not only that race is unimportant, but that it counts for absolutely nothing. And it is a little strange that Herr Barth refers to the words of some unnamed English statesman, while he will of course have read in the works of the world famous English philosopher, John Stuart Mill, about the assumption of racial differences: 'Of all vulgar modes of escaping from the consideration of the effect of social and moral influences on the human mind the most vulgar is that of attributing the diversities of conduct and character to inherent natural differences.' (*Principles of Political Economy* Vol. 1, p. 390.)

Historical materialism does not neglect race in any way: it is the first to make it a clear concept. There is no more an unchanging race of human beings than there is an unchanging race of animals, except that animals are subject to the laws of development of nature, and the human race is subject to the laws of development of society. The more human beings become independent of nature, the more the natural races mix and merge together; the more man's control over nature grows, the more completely the natural races become transformed into social classes. And as far as the capitalist mode of production extends, the differences between the races have been dissolved or are dissolving more each day into the class opposites. Within human society race is not a natural but a historic concept, which in the last analysis is determined by the material form of production, and is subordinate to the laws of its development, as Kautsky proved in the most convincing way in relation to concepts of nationality.[39]

But just like those conditions which are to be traced back to human nature, so the natural external conditions of work too are incorporated in the social process of production. If Herr Barth speaks especially of climate, then he does so remembering that Montesquieu tried to make climate the lever of political history, that Winckelmann applied the same principle to the history of art, Harder to the history of culture, although with some diversions, reservations and extensions, and that in our century Buckle derived human history from the two-sided relationship between on the one hand the human spirit, and on the other climate, food, the land and other natural phenomena. And certainly this theory was a remarkable advance as opposed to the theological or the rationalistic conception of history, however much Hegel may have said: 'Don't talk to me about the climate, since the Turks now live where the Greeks used to,' and Bobineau may have attempted to deny any influence of the climate on the development of history. If however Hegel tries to make the absolute idea the lever of historical development and Govineau tries to use the different mixtures of blood, then they represent to say the least no advance on the conception of history advanced from Montesquieu to Buckle. But in any case, to stick to the most consistent representative of the whole tendency, Buckle overlooked precisely the decisive point, the missing link, which makes a whole out of the two halves, which makes his dualist outlook a monist one: the mode of production of material life, which brings together mind and nature, which alone makes the human mind capable of winning control over nature, and can wrest nature's secrets from it, to make them productive forces in the hands of men. This, which Buckle did not recognize, is what historical materialism emphasizes as the decisive point, and if we have already seen that it in no way denies the laws of the mind, we cannot understand either how it can deny the laws of nature or even the laws of the climate. When did historical materialism claim that cultivation could be carried out on the icebergs of the North Pole, or that it was possible to sail boats on the sand dunes of the Sahara desert? On the contrary, Marx gave the most careful consideration to the significance of natural forces in relation to human production. This is what he writes, to quote one more example:

> Capitalist production once assumed, then, all other circumstances remaining the same, and given the length of the working-day, the quantity of surplus-labour will vary with the physical conditions of labour, especially with the fertility of the soil. But it by no means follows from this that the most fruitful soil is the most fitted for the growth of the capitalist mode of production. This mode is based on the dominion of man over Nature. Where Nature is too lavish, she 'keeps him in hand, like a child in leading-strings'. She does not impose upon him any necessity to develop himself. It is not the tropics with their luxuriant vegetation, but the temperate zone, that is the mother-country of capital. It is not the mere fertility of the soil, but the differentiation of the soil, the variety of its natural products, the changes of the seasons, which form the physical basis for the social division of labour, and which, by changes in his natural surroundings, spur man on to the multiplication of his wants, his capabilities, his means and modes of labour. It is the necessity of bringing a natural force under the control of society, of economizing, of appropriating or subduing it on a large scale by the work of man's hand, that first plays the decisive part in the history of industry.[40]

This one passage, not to mention countless others, already shows how far Marx's theory of history 'neglects' the natural elements and the climate.

But wherever nature allows the existence of man and the unfolding of a social process of production, there the natural conditions of work are subsumed into this process; they are taken up by it, changed and subdued, and they lose significance to the same degree that the control of man over nature increases. They play their role in the history of human society only through the process of production, and therefore it is quite enough for Marx to say that the mode of production of material life determines the process of social, political and intellectual life in general. In each mode of production, the relevant natural conditioning of the work is contained, and beyond this nature plays no further role in the history of human society. This means, in other words, that the same form of production determines the social process of life in the same way, be the climate, race and other natural conditions as varied as they like, and different modes of production determine the social process of life differently where climate, race and the other natural conditions of life are completely similar. To take one historical example of each to prove these two propositions, and in fact strengthen them, permit us to draw these examples not from the conditions of civilization, where the domination of man over nature is more or less advanced, but from barbaric conditions, where man is almost completely dominated by nature which stands opposed to him, hostile and incomprehensible.

> One finds in all peoples with collective property, despite the differences of race and climate, exactly the same vices, passions and virtues, almost identical habits and forms of thought. Artificial conditions call forth the same phenomena in races formed differently by natural conditions.[41]

Thus wrote Lafargue, who in this connection understands social conditions as being part of the artificial conditions.

He is quoted here precisely because he makes particular reference to race and climate; and in the writings of Morgan, Engels, Kautsky and others there are many illustrations of how among all 'peoples with collective property', that is, in all gentile societies in the past, the whole process of life takes place in the same way. Moreover Herr Barth himself speaks elsewhere in his work of the 'similarity of all societies' at the beginning of culture, and refers specifically to Morgan's major epoch-making work, in which, however, he does not appear to have got wind of the devil's brew of historical materialism. But if Morgan, according to Herr Barth, proves the gentile constitution of the greatest part of the earth from China westward towards North America, 'and assumes it correctly for the small remaining part, for which he has not yet found proof' — what then do climate and race have to do with the history of human society, where this society is still firmly tied to the umbilical cord of nature?

It is necessary here to mention a very remarkable example which shows how with complete equality of climate and race, different modes of production determine the whole life process in a different way. It comes from the writings of a famous American traveller, Kennan, who, with his clear vision, and straightforward understanding, had already, as a young man of twenty years old, discovered historical materialism after his own fashion without ever having heard of Marx and Engels or even of his fellow-countryman, Morgan.[42] In the northern part of the Kamchatka peninsula, more or less the most inhospitable part of the inhabited earth, live the Koryaks, a tribe consisting of about forty patriarchal families, who make their living through the training and breeding of reindeer. They are forced into a nomadic form of life through this mode of production.

> A herd of four or five thousand reindeer will, in a very few days, paw up the snow and eat all the moss within a radius of a mile from the encampment, and then, of course, the band must move to fresh ground.... They [the Koryaks] *must* wander or their deer will starve, and then their own starvation follows as a natural consequence.

How dependent the mode of production of the Koryaks is on nature is reflected in their childlike religious conceptions. Their only religion is the worship of evil spirits. The priests of this religion have to let themselves be whipped thoroughly in order to prove the genuine nature of their revelations; if they withstand their chastisement without any signs of weakness they are recognized as servants of the evil spirits and their orders are followed despite all the hocus-pocus that they deceive others into believing and themselves into carrying out, such as the swallowing of live coals and similar mad acts.

> It is the only religion possible for such men in such circumstances.... If a band of ignorant, barbarous Mahometans were transported to North-Eastern Siberia — compelled to live in tents, century after century, amid the wild, gloomy scenery of the Stanavoi Mountains, to suffer terrific storms whose causes they could not explain, to lose their reindeer suddenly by an epidemic disease which defied human remedies, to be frightened by magnificent auroras that set the whole universe ablaze, and decimated by pestilences whose nature they could not understand, and whose disastrous effects they were powerless to avert — they would almost inevitably lose by degrees their faith in Allah-Mahomet, and become precisely such Shamanists as the Siberian Koryaks.

The Russian Church is making efforts to convert all the Siberian heathens into Christians, but their missionaries are having a degree of success only with the settled tribes; all their efforts bounce off the migrant Koryaks without a trace, and Kennan says correctly that the conversion of these nomads would have to be preceded by a total upheaval of their mode of life, that is to say the mode of production.

This form of production not only ties the Koryaks down to childlike religious concepts but also forces them into barbaric habits, to deny what Kennan calls 'the strongest emotions of human nature'. They kill all elderly people; they impale the sick or stone them to death if they have no hope that they will get better; they know how to explain the different forms of killing with 'the most sickening minuteness'. But all the Koryaks see a natural end to existence in the death of a man or woman by the hand of a close relative; no-one wants it to be any different.

> The barrenness of the soil in North-Eastern Siberia, and the severity of the long winter, led men to domesticate the reindeer as the only means of obtaining a subsistence; the domestication of the reindeer necessitated a wandering life; a wandering life made sickness and infirmity unusually burdensome to both sufferers and supporters; and this finally led to the murder of the old and the sick, as a measure both of policy and mercy.

And Kennan again correctly points out that this ugly custom did not mean that the Koryaks were innately backward by origin. It is the result of the same mode of production which made the nomadic Koryaks an honest, hospitable, generous, bold and independent breed of men. The Koryaks treat their wives and children with great kindness; during his more than two years of contact with them Kennan never saw a woman or a child being beaten, and he himself was treated with 'as much kindness and generous hospitality' as he had ever experienced in a civilized country with Christian inhabitants.

Now some three or four hundred Koryaks lost their reindeer through a pestilence, and were thus forced to lead a sedentary life. They live in houses made of driftwood on the sea-coast and live by fishing and hunting seals; they also hunt for whale-bones, which have had their blubber removed by American whalers and wash up on the sea-shore. They are engaged in trade with Russian peasants and traders and with American whalers. Let us listen to Kennan as he explains how this changed mode of production changed the whole life-process of the Koryaks! He writes:

> The settled Koryaks of Penzhinsk Gulf are unquestionably the worst, ugliest, most brutal, degraded natives in all North-Eastern Siberia...they are cruel and brutal in disposition, insolent to everybody, revengeful, dishonest and untruthful. Everything which the wandering Koryaks are, they are not.

And he shows in detail how these changes are due to the sedentary Koryaks' trade and concludes:

> I have a very sincere and hearty admiration for many wandering Koryaks ...but their settled relatives are the worst specimens of men that I ever saw in all Northern Asia, from Bering's Straits to the Ural mountains.

And yet, as far as climate and race and all other natural conditions are concerned, even a magnifying glass would not find the slightest trace of difference between the sedentary and the migrant Koryaks. But enough of these aphoristic remarks, which, to repeat once again, are not an exhaustive exposition of historical materialism, but are only intended to refute arguments which have been raised against it. Whoever wants to get to know it completely, must study the works of Marx, Engels, Morgan, Kautsky, Dietzgen, Buerkli, Lafargue, Plekhanov, and the files of *Neue Zeit*. With regard to these works, Engels could well say that the proof of the correctness of the materialist investigation of history had been shown, and that if Herr Barth complains that Engels 'unfortunately' does not name these works to which he refers, then our learned friend is overlooking the fact that Engels does not write for German university professors, but for thinking workers. If Engels were writing for German professors, then he would perhaps — who knows? — be so generous as to go into the matter more closely than is necessary for thinking workers.

If one can then say that historical materialism has a firm and indestructible basis, this is not to say that every result of its analysis is completely indisputable, nor that there is nothing left for it to do. Where the materialist examination of history is misused as a *model*, then it leads to the same distortions as the use of any model in the study of history, and even where it is correctly applied as a *method*, the different talent or education of those who apply it, or the difference in the nature and extent of the source material which is at their disposal, leads to many differences in conception. This is quite obvious, since in the field of history a mathematically precise proof is just not possible, and whoever tries to challenge the materialist method of research into history because of such contradictions, should not be further disturbed in his or her bird-brained pleasures. For reasonable people, 'contradictions' of this kind will only serve as an opportunity to test which of the mutually contradictory researchers has carried out his investigations more accurately and more thoroughly. Thus the method itself can only gain clarity and certainty, in its application as in its conclusions, from precisely these 'contradictions'.

There is still infinitely much for historical materialism to do until it has shed light on the history of humanity in its innumerable ramifications, and its greatest power will never unfold on the terrain of bourgeois society because its growing strength will first of all smash this society. It must certainly be recognized that the conscientious historians of the bourgeoisie are to some extent under the influence of historical materialism, as we have noted repeatedly in this sketch, although this influence is always confined within certain limits.

As long as there is a bourgeois class, it cannot give up bourgeois ideology, and even Lamprecht, the most renowned representative of the trend of so-called 'economic history', begins his *History of Germany* with a basic outline, not of the German economy, but of 'German national consciousness'. Historical idealism in its most varied theological, rationalistic and also naturalist manifestations is the historical conception of the bourgeois class, just as historical materialism is the historical outlook of the working class. Only with the emancipation of the proletariat will it come to full flower, and will history become a science in the strict sense of the word — what it always ought to have been but has never yet been: a teacher and leader of humanity.

APPENDIX

Letter from Engels to Franz Mehring in Berlin

London, July 14, 1893

Dear Herr Mehring,

Today is my first opportunity to thank you for the *Lessing Legend* you were kind enough to send me. I did not want to reply with a bare formal acknowledgment of receipt of the book but intended at the same time to tell you something about it, about its contents. Hence the delay.

I shall begin at the end — the appendix on historical materialism, in which you have lined up the main things excellently and for any unprejudiced person convincingly. If I find anything to object to it is that you give me more credit than I deserve, even if I count in everything which I might possibly have found out for myself — in time — but which Marx with his more rapid *coup d'oeil* and wider vision discovered much more quickly. When one had the good fortune to work for forty years with a man like Marx, one usually does not during his lifetime get the recognition one thinks one deserves. Then, when the greater man dies, the lesser easily gets overrated and this seems to me to be just my case at present; history will set all this right in the end and by that time one will have quietly turned up one's toes and not know anything any more about anything.

Otherwise only one more point is lacking, which, however, Marx and I always failed to stress enough in our writings and in regard to which we are all equally guilty. That is to say, we all laid, and *were bound* to lay, the main emphasis, in the first place, on the *derivation* of political, juridical and other ideological notions, and of actions arising through the medium of these notions, from basic economic facts. But in so doing we neglected the formal side — the ways and means by which these notions, etc., come about — for the sake of the content. This has given our adversaries a welcome opportunity for misunderstandings and distortions, of which Paul Barth is a striking example.

Ideology is a process accomplished by the so-called thinker consciously, it is true, but with a false consciousness. The real motive forces impelling him remain unknown to him; otherwise it simply would not be an ideological process. Hence he imagines false or seeming motive forces. Because it is a process of thought he derives its form as well as its content from pure thought, either his own or that of his predecessors. He works with mere thought material, which he accepts without examination as the product of thought, and does not investigate further for a more remote source independent of thought; indeed this is a matter of course to him, because, as all action is *mediated* by thought, it appears to him to be ultimately *based* upon thought.

The historical ideologist (historical is here simply meant to comprise the political, juridical, philosophical, theological — in short, all the spheres belonging to *society* and not only to nature) thus possesses in every sphere of science material which has formed itself independently out of the thought of previous generations and has gone through its own independent course of development in the brains of these successive generations. True, external facts belonging to one or another sphere may have exercised a codetermining influence on this development, but the tacit presupposition is that these facts themselves are also only the fruits of a process of thought, and so we still remain within that realm of mere thought, which apparently has successfully digested even the hardest facts.

It is above all this semblance of an independent history of state constitutions, of systems of law, of ideological conceptions in every separate domain that dazzles most people. If Luther and Calvin 'overcome' the official Catholic religion or Hegel 'overcomes' Fichte and Kant or Rousseau with his republican *Contrat social* indirectly 'overcomes' the constitutional Montesquieu, this is a process which remains within theology, philosophy or political science, represents a stage in the history of these particular spheres of thought and never passes beyond the sphere of thought. And since the bourgeois illusion of the eternity and finality of capitalist production has been added as well, even the overcoming of the mercantilists by the physiocrats and Adam Smith is accounted as a sheer victory of thought; not as the reflection in thought of changed economic facts but as the finally achieved correct understanding of actual conditions subsisting always and everywhere — in fact, if Richard Coeur-de-Lion and Philip Augustus had introduced free trade instead of getting mixed up in the crusades we should have been spared five hundred years of misery and stupidity.

This aspect of the matter, which I can only indicate here, we have all, I think, neglected more than it deserves. It is the old story: form is always neglected at first for content. As I say, I have done that too and the mistake has always struck me only later. So I am not only far from reproaching you with this in any way — as the older of the guilty parties I certainly have no right to do so; on the contrary. But I would like all the same to draw your attention to this point for the future.

Hanging together with this is the fatuous notion of the ideologists that because we deny an independent historical development to the various ideological spheres which play a part in history we also deny them any *effect upon history.* The basis of this is the common undialectical conception of cause and effect as rigidly opposite poles, the total disregarding of interaction. These gentlemen often almost deliberately forget that once an historic element has been brought into the world by other, ultimately economic causes, it reacts, can react on its environment and even on the causes that have given rise to it. For instance, Barth on the priesthood and religion, your page 475. I was very glad to see how you settled this fellow, whose banality exceeds all expectations; and him they make professor of history in Leipzig! I must say that old man Wachsmuth — also rather a bonehead but greatly appreciative of facts — was quite a different chap.

As for the rest, I can only repeat about the book what I repeatedly said about the articles when they appeared in the *Neue Zeit:* it is by far the best presentation in existence of the genesis of the Prussian state.* Indeed, I may well say that it is the only good presentation, correctly developing in most matters their interconnections down to the veriest details. One regrets only that you were unable to include the entire further development down to Bismarck and one hopes involuntarily that you will do this another time and present a complete coherent picture, from the Elector Frederick William down to old William. You have already made your preliminary investigations and, in the main at least, they are as good as finished. The thing has to be done sometime anyhow before the shaky old shanty comes tumbling down. The dissipation of the monarchical-patriotic legends, while not directly a necessary preliminary for the abolition of the monarchy which screens class domination (inasmuch as a *pure*, bourgeois republic in Germany was outstripped by events before it came into existence) will nevertheless be one of the most effective levers for that purpose.

Then you will have more space and opportunity to depict the local history of Prussia as part of the general misery that Germany has gone through. This is the point where I occasionally depart somewhat from your view, especially in the conception of the preliminary conditions for the dismemberment of Germany and of the failure of the bourgeois revolution in Germany during the sixteenth century. When I get down to reworking the historical introduction to my *Peasant War*, which I hope will be next winter, I shall be able to develop there the points in question. Not that I consider those you indicated incorrect, but I put others alongside them and group them somewhat differently.

In studying German history — the story of a continuous state of wretchedness — I have always found that only a comparison with the corresponding French periods produces a correct idea of proportions, because what happens there is the direct opposite of what happens in our country. There, the establishment of a national state from the scattered parts of the feudal state precisely at the time we pass through the period of our greatest decline. There, a rare objective logic during the whole course of the process; with us,

* See F. Mehring, *Absolutism and Revolution in Germany 1525-1848* (New Park Publications, 1975).

more and more dismal dislocation. There, during the Middle Ages, foreign intervention is represented by the English conqueror who intervenes in favour of the Provençal nationality against the Northern French nationality. The wars with England represent, in a way, the Thirty Years' War, which, however, ends in the ejection of the foreign invaders and the subjugation of the South by the North. Then comes the struggle between the central power and vassal Burgundy, supported by its foreign possessions, which plays the part of Brandenburg-Prussia, a struggle which ends, however, in the victory of the central power and conclusively establishes the national state. And precisely at that moment the national state completely collapses in our country (in so far as the 'German kingdom' within the Holy Roman Empire can be called a national state) and the plundering of German territory on a large scale sets in. This comparison is most humiliating for Germans but for that very reason the more instructive; and since our workers have put Germany back again the forefront of the historical movement it has become somewhat easier for us to swallow the ignominy of the past.

Another especially significant feature of the development of Germany is the fact that neither of the partial states which in the end partitioned Germany between them was purely German — both were colonies on conquered Slav territory: Austria a Bavarian and Brandenburg a Saxon colony — and that they acquired power *within* Germany only by relying upon the support of foreign, non-German possessions: Austria upon that of Hungary (not to mention Bohemia) and Brandenburg that of Prussia. On the Western border, the one in greatest jeopardy, nothing of the kind took place; on the Northern border it was left to the Danes to protect Germany against the Danes; and in the South there was so little to protect that the frontier guard, the Swiss, even succeeded in tearing themselves loose from Germany!

But I have allowed myself to drift into all kinds of extraneous matter. Let this palaver at least serve you as proof of how stimulating an effect your work has upon me.

Once more cordial thanks and greetings from

Yours,
F. Engels

Explanatory Notes

[1] Engels, *Ludwig Feuerbach and the End of the Classical German Philosophy*, Marx-Engels Selected Works p. 614 [One-volume edition, Lawrence and Wishart, 1968, hereafter MESW]

[2] To be just we must point out explicitly that a few bourgeois historical researchers are trying to adopt a less biased attitude twoards the materialist theory of history. Thus the *Jahresberichte der Geschichtswissenschaft* (*Annals of Historical Science*) published by Jastrow register the second volume of *Capital* as a very important work particularly for the historical science, and in the *Historische Zeitschrift*, No. 68, p. 450, Paul Hinneberg says in a critique 'that works like Morgan's *Ancient Society* and Bachofen's *Mutterrecht* are audibly knocking at the gates of science'. To this, however, the editor, Herr Max Lehmann, Professor of History at Leipzig, adds the witty note: 'We regret that here and there a colleague is listening to this knocking; we, that is to say, leave Herr Morgan outside. Let him provide Herren Engels and Bebel with the portion of alleged knowledge they think indispensable to give their theories some foundation'. That is, as far as we can see, the only mention of historical materialism in the more than seventy volumes of the *Historische Zeitschrift*, the chief organ of bourgeois historical science! [Note by Mehring]

[3] Marx, Preface to *A Contribution to the Critique of Political Economy*, MESW p. 182.

[4] Marx and Engels, *Communist Manifesto*, MESW pp. 35-36.

[5] *MESW* p. 429.

[6] Lavergne-Peghuilen, *Die Bewegungs-und Productionsgesetze*, p. 225

[7] Engels to Mehring, September 1892. Marx-Engels *Selected Correspondence*, pp. 449-450.

[8] Engels, *Ludwig Feuerbach, MESW*, pp. 600-601.

[9] Hellwald, *Kulturgeschichte in ihrer natürlichen Entwicklung*, p. 688, 689f.

[10] Bourgeois sociologists such as Herbert Spencer claim in all seriousness, as we know, that man is indeed an isolated creation of nature. They speak of his 'individual activity in his primitive condition'. But what we have here is only a Darwinistically embellished re-issue of the doctrine of the Social Contract, which in the seventeenth and eighteenth centuries the ideologists of the rising bourgeoisie from Hobbes to Rousseau transferred

from the rise of the modern state out of the treaties concluded between the Princes and the towns to subdue feudal anarchy, to the rise of human society. On this see Kautsky, 'Die sozialen Triebe in der Menschenwelt', *Neue Zeit*, 2nd Year, p. 13ff. [Note by Mehring].

[11] Adolf Wagner, *Das neue sozialdemokratische Programm*, p. 9f. We have taken the liberty of dissecting Herr Wagner's nonsense a little in *Neue Zeit*, 10th Year, vol. 2, p. 577ff. [Note by Mehring].

[12] *Vorwärts*, October 5, 1890.

[13] Kautsky, *Die Klassengegensätze von 1789*.

[14] Engels, Preface to the German Edition of *Socialism, Utopian and Scientific*.

[15] Marx, *Capital*, Afterword to the Second German Edition, Moscow, 1961, p. 20.

[16] Marx, Preface to *A Contribution to the Critique of Political Economy*, MESW p. 182, and Engels, *Socialism Utopian and Scientific*, MESW p. 426.

[17] Lewis H. Morgan, *Ancient Society*, Part 1 Chapter 2.

[18] Engels, *The Origins of the Family, Private Property and the State*, IX, 'Barbarism and Civilization', *MESW* pp. 566-83.

[19] Morgan writes: 'The phonetic alphabet came, like other great inventions, at the end of successive efforts'. (Note to Part 1 Chapter 3 of *Ancient Society*.). See also Karl Marx, *Capital*, note on p. 372: 'A critical history of technology would show how little any of the inventions of the eighteenth century are the work of a single individual'. [Note by Mehring].

[20] Marx, *Capital*, vol. 1, p. 428.

[21] Delbrück *Historische und politische Aufsätze*, p. 339ff.

[23] On this see the splendid books by Karl Bürkli, *Der wahre Winkelried, die Taktik der Urschweizer*, and *Der Ursprung der Eidgenossenschaft aus der Markgenossenschaft und die Schlacht am Morgarten*. [Note by Mehring].

[24] Paul Barth, *Die Geschichtsphilosophie Hegels und der Hegelianer bis auf Marx und Hartmann*, p. 70ff.

[25] Lamprecht, *Deutsche Geschichte*, vol. 2, p. 89ff.

[26] See Mehring, *Absolutism and Revolution in Germany*, Chapter 1, 'The German Reformation and its consequences.'

[27] For a description of this early form of land ownership see Engels' article 'The Mark' published as an appendix in *The Peasant War in Germany*, Lawrence and Wishart 1969.

[28] Treitschke, *Deutsche Kämpfe*, p. 516.

[29] Marx, *Capital*, Vol. I, Moscow 1961, note on p. 514.

³⁰ Metschnikoff, *La civilisation et les grands fleuves historiques*, p. 189. See also Plekhanov's critical review of this work in *Neue Zeit* 9th Year, vol. 1, p. 437ff. [Note by Mehring].

³¹ Kautsky, *Thomas More and his Utopia*, p. 80ff.

³² Liebknecht, *Zur orientalischen Frage*, p. 57.

³³ Apart from Marx's indications and expositions scattered through *Capital*, cf. on the origins of Christianity Engels, *Bruno Bauer und das Urchristentum*, in the Zurich *Sozialdemokrat* 1882 Nos. 19 and 20, [in English in Marx and Engels *On Religion*] and Kautsky, *Die Entstehung des Christentums* in *Neue Zeit*, 3rd Year, p. 481ff. On the medieval church and the Protestant reformist movement that developed out of it, see Engel's writings on the Peasant War in Germany and on Feuerbach, and also Kautsky's book on Thomas More; countless other essays in the *Neue Zeit* of which we must particularly mention Engels, *Über historischen Materialismus*, 11th Year, vol. 1, p. 15 ff, and the anonymous essay on *Juristen-Sozialismus*, 5th Year, p. 49 ff., and also Kautsky, *Die Bergarbeiter und der Bauernkrieg*, 7th Year, p. 289 ff., and more recently the same author's *Zukunftsstaaten der Vergangenheit*, 11th year vol. 1, p. 653 ff. On the scientific materialist criticism of the Old Testament we must also mention Lafargue, *Der Mythus von Adam und Eva*, 9th Year vol. 2, p. 225 ff., and M. Beer, *Ein Beitrag zur Geschichte des Klassenkampfes im hebräischen Altertum* 11th year, vol. 1, p. 444 ff., and also Kautsky, *Die Entstehung der biblischen Urgeschichte im Kosmos*, 7th Year, p. 201 ff. [Note by Mehring].

³⁴ Giesebrecht, *Geschichte der deutschen Kaiserzeit*, vol. 2 p. 36.

³⁵ 'Are *carefully* ignored and overlooked'! as Herr Barth most recently says, raising the same objection against Engels in *Deutsche Worte*. [Note by Mehring.]

³⁶ Dietzgen, *The Nature of Human Brain-Work*.

³⁷ Gumplowicz, *Der Rassenkampf*, p. 184. How far this in any case very stimulating book is in agreement with historical materialism or not is discussed in detail by Kautsky in the *Neue Zeit*, 1st Year, p. 537 ff. [Note by Mehring]

³⁸ J.S. Mill, *Principles of Political Economy*, Vol. 1 p. 390 (in the second edition of 1849).

³⁹ Kautsky, *Die moderne Nationalität*, in *Neue Zeit*, 5th Year, p. 392ff. See also *ibid*. p. 187ff. Guido Hammer's essay on the disruption of the modern nationalities. [Note by Mehring.]

⁴⁰ Marx, *Capital*, vol 1 pp. 513-514, Moscow 1961.

⁴¹ Lafargue, *Der wirtschaftliche Materialismus nach den Anschauungen von Karl Marx*, p. 32.

⁴² George Kennan, *Tent Life in Siberia and Adventures among the Koryaks and Other Tribes in Kamtchatka and Northern Asia*, London 1871. p. 124 ff.